Hand Me Another Brick:
Timeless Lessons on Leadership

How Effective Leaders Motivate Themselves and Others

FOR YOU, TAMMEE...
WITH GRATITUDE
FOR YOUR LIFE!

Chuck Swindoll

Active Spirituality
Bedside Blessings
Behold . . . The Man!
The Bride
Come Before Winter
Compassion: Showing We Care in a
  Careless World
The Darkness and the Dawn
David: A Man of Passion and Destiny
Day by Day
Dear Graduate
Dropping Your Guard
Elijah: A Man of Heroism and Humility
Encourage Me
Esther: A Woman of Strength and Dignity
Fascinating Stories of Forgotten Lives
Fascinating Stories of Forgotten Lives
  Workbook
The Finishing Touch
Five Meaningful Minutes a Day
Flying Closer to the Flame
For Those Who Hurt
Getting Through the Tough Stuff
Getting Through the Tough Stuff
  Workbook
God's Provision
The Grace Awakening
The Grace Awakening Devotional
The Grace Awakening Workbook
Great Attitudes!
Great Days with Great Lives
Growing Deep in the Christian Life
Growing Strong in the Seasons of Life
Growing Wise in Family Life
Hand Me Another Brick: Timeless
  Lessons on Leadership
Hand Me Another Brick Bible Companion
Home: Where Life Makes Up Its Mind
Hope Again
Improving Your Serve
Intimacy with the Almighty

Job: A Man of Heroic Endurance
Job: Interactive Study Guide
Joseph: A Man of Integrity and
  Forgiveness
Killing Giants, Pulling Thorns
Laugh Again
Leadership: Influence That Inspires
Living Above the Level of Mediocrity
Living Beyond the Daily Grind,
  Books I and II
The Living Insight Study Bible,
  general editor
Living on the Ragged Edge
Living on the Ragged Edge Workbook
Make Up Your Mind
Man to Man
Marriage: From Surviving to Thriving
Marriage: From Surviving to Thriving
  Workbook
Moses: A Man of Selfless Dedication
The Mystery of God's Will
Parenting: From Surviving to Thriving
Parenting: From Surviving to Thriving
  Workbook
Paul: A Man of Grace and Grit
The Quest for Character
Recovery: When Healing Takes Time
The Road to Armageddon
Sanctity of Life
Shedding Light on Our Dark Side
Simple Faith
Simple Trust
So, You Want to Be Like Christ?
So, You Want to Be Like Christ? Workbook
Starting Over
Start Where You Are
Strengthening Your Grip
Stress Fractures
Strike the Original Match
The Strong Family
Suddenly One Morning

Hand Me Another Brick:
Timeless Lessons on Leadership

*How Effective Leaders Motivate
Themselves and Others*

BY

CHARLES R. SWINDOLL

W PUBLISHING GROUP
A Division of Thomas Nelson Publishers
Since 1798

www.wpublishinggroup.com

HAND ME ANOTHER BRICK: TIMELESS LESSONS ON LEADERSHIP
How Effective Leaders Motivate Themselves and Others

Published by W Publishing Group, a division of Thomas Nelson, Inc., Post Office Box 141000, Nashville, Tennessee, 37214.

Unless otherwise identified, Scripture quotations are from the New American Standard ® Bible (NASB). Copyright © 1960, 1962, 1963, 1968, 1971, 1972, 1973, 1975, 1977, 1995 by The Lockman Foundation, La Habra, CA. Used by permission. All rights reserved. (www.Lockman.org)

Other Scripture references are from The Modern Language Bible. The New Berkeley Version in Modern English, Revised Version (MLB). © 1945, 1959, 1969 by Hendrickson Publishers, Inc. The Message (MSG), copyright © 1993. Used by permission of NavPress Publishing Group.

Editorial Staff: David Moberg, acquisitions editor, and Thom Chittom, managing editor
Cover Design: Tobias' Outerwear for Books

W Publishing Group books may be purchased in bulk for educational, business, fund-raising, or sales promotional use. For information, please email: SpecialMarkets@ThomasNelson.com.

Library of Congress Cataloging-in-Publication Data

Swindoll, Charles R.
  Hand me another brick / Charles R. Swindoll.
    p. cm.
  ISBN–10: 0-8499-1460-4 (trade paper)
  ISBN–13: 978-0-8499-1460-7 (trade paper)

  1. Christian leadership. 2. Leadership—Biblical teaching. 3. Bible.
O.T. Nehemiah—Criticism, interpretation, etc. 4. Nehemiah (Governnor of Judah) I. Title.

BV652.1.S94   2007
262'.1—dc22   2006035887

Printed in the United States of America
07 08 09 10 11 RRD 5 4 3 2 1

This book is gratefully dedicated to the men on my staff whose loyalty I appreciate and whose leadership I admire.
Each man models the message of this book.

CONTENTS

Contents

INTRODUCTION

This is a practical book about leadership. My desire is threefold: (1) to be accurate with the facts as they relate to leadership and to Scripture, (2) to be clear, that is, nontechnical and free from meaningless clichés, and (3) to be relevant and current in my comments, explaining how these ideas and suggestions can be implemented.

This is not a book of theory. I will leave the philosophical and psychological aspects of leadership and character development to the experts on the subject. My approach grows out of realistic observations I have made over the past fifty-plus years in various areas of personal experience: a tour of duty in the U.S. Marine Corps (military leadership); several years in graduate school (educational leadership); employment in industry and business (labor and corporation leadership); more than four decades in churches, both in America and abroad (ecclesiastical leadership); and as a husband, father of four children, and grandfather to ten (domestic leadership).

As a student of the Bible, I continue to uncover more and more truth on this vital subject. It seems a shame to keep it hidden in my head or tucked away in my files, especially with so little being communicated about leadership from a scriptural perspective. Because I am convinced of the profound and powerful impact the Bible brings to those who glean its wisdom, I share these insights with genuine excitement.

My hope is to reach a broad cross section of today's world—from the up-and-coming young person who is stimulated with the thought of leading others, to the top executive who lives in the threatening arena of difficult decisions and exhausting demands. It is out of a deep respect for these men and women, whose spheres of influence require long hours and disciplined thinking, that I write these words.

Being a leader is an unenviable calling. It appears glamorous and glorious to the novice, but it is more often lonely and thankless. As we shall see, the best leaders are actually servants. Unselfishly, they give of themselves to accomplish the objectives, regardless of the sacrifice or cost. The perils are ever present, the criticism is relentless, and the toll is great. But so are the rewards, fleeting though they may seem.

Originally, I presented the material in this book to the attentive and responsive congregation of the church I served as senior pastor, then I shared the insights in a number of Bible conferences, on scores of Christian college campuses and at seminars dealing with leadership. I cannot remember a time following such occasions when individuals did not urge me to make the series available in book form. Originally, I published this book in 1973. I'm grateful that my publisher urged me to return to these pages and revise them for today's readers.

I appreciate, more than words can say, the editorial acumen of Mark Gaither, whose talent and diligence proved invaluable. I remain indebted to Helen Peters for her secretarial assistance in transcribing the original material and typing the final manuscript with such personal interest, remarkable speed, and devoted concern. And to my wife, Cynthia, a constant partner, my source of stimulating encouragement and penetrating discussions, I freely declare my gratitude. Only she knows the relentless process of rewriting these original pages in light of our twenty-first-century world, where great leadership is needed more than ever.

To God be the glory.

Chuck Swindoll

Frisco, Texas

ONE

The Matter at Hand

Glance through today's newspaper and chances are good you will find another story of leadership breakdown. In my native state of Texas, thousands of Enron Corporation employees face financial ruin as a result of poor—even corrupt—leadership. They trusted their leaders to properly steward the money they had invested with their employer for retirement, literally banking on their leaders. However, even as one popular financial news magazine named Enron "America's Most Innovative Company" several years in a row, executives and accountants were busy using "creative accounting" tricks to inflate the company's assets while shifting debts to offshore subsidiaries. When the financial shell game was over, Enron's loyal employees came out the losers. Bottom line: Enron's failure was the result of a complete breakdown in leadership.

A similar scene exists today in many churches, Christian organizations, and educational institutions. Although things may appear smooth and stable on the surface, beneath the thin veneer it is not unusual to find internal strife or organizational confusion. Too often the standards of ethics and practice that define secular money-and-power organizations are cleverly sanctified and adapted to the spiritual realm. It's always a bad fit, and never something that should characterize the Christian leader, regardless of what kind of enterprise he or she leads.

So much of our personal frustration in daily living comes as a direct result of faulty leadership—personality conflicts, communication breakdowns, incompetence, power struggles, poor management of time and resources, and poorly defined roles and responsibilities. Our responsibilities are so much easier to bear when we have good leadership, and so burdensome under poor leadership. The crying need for accomplished leaders could not be louder or clearer.

What is a Leader?

What do we mean when we use the word *leadership*? If I were to define it in a single word, I would choose the term "influence." You lead someone to the degree you influence him or her.

The late President Harry Truman often referred to leaders as people who can get others to do what they don't want to do—and get them to enjoy doing it!

Reams of pages and stacks of books have been penned on the subject of leadership. Dale Carnegie's *How to Win Friends and Influence People*, a landmark volume on leadership and personal relationships, is still required reading in many MBA programs. Stephen R. Covey's *The 7 Habits of Highly Effective People* has become a modern classic. Even books such as *The One-Minute Manager* and, one of my favorites, *How to Develop the Leader Within You,* relate to leadership by addressing the subject of handling person-to-person encounters. But all of these leadership manuals sit in the shadow of another, more ancient volume.

A Manual for Leaders

One book, written about 425 BC, still stands as a classic work on effective leadership; yet it is strangely obscure and virtually unknown to people today. It was written by a man who was prominent in business and politics in the ancient Middle East. He not only possessed an exceptional personal philosophy of leadership, but he *lived it out* as well. In his lifetime, this gentleman rose from utter obscurity to national recognition. The book he penned bears his name: Nehemiah.

Believe it or not, what Nehemiah had to say concerning leadership speaks to the very same issues you and I face today. For example, from his book we learn

- how to relate to a touchy boss;

- how to balance faith in God's sovereignty and the need for personal planning;

- how to handle discouragement at the executive level; and

- how to respond to unwarranted criticism.

In this biblical manual for leaders we find timeless and reliable guidelines that work. They enable us to know how to build quality characteristics in ourselves and others—the kind that are rarely seen today. These truths are not suddenly "dumped" on us, but rather handed to us—brick by brick, as it were—in the form of a narrative. The story begins with an unassuming servant and follows his personal journey to become the official governor of Israel during its reconstruction, which incidentally points us to our first lesson. Good leaders are made, not born; they are built, shaped, and tested by God—brick by brick—over time.

That's the purpose of this ancient book: to equip you, to build you into the kind of leader God desires—a true leader. If you allow yourself to get caught up in the story, you will find something wonderful begin to happen. As you watch the plot develop, as you see Nehemiah's character and his project built, shaped, and tested, you will find something in your hand that wasn't there before: a brick, something with which to begin building your own character.

Whatever you do, don't just stand there. Use it. Set it in place and continue reading. And before the end of the story, I think you will be amazed by how many bricks were passed from Nehemiah's hands to yours.

A Man to Match the Mountain

As far as leadership traits are concerned, Nehemiah was not that different from outstanding people whose names are far more familiar to us. Our nation's twenty-sixth president, for example, was a hard-charging leader. Throughout his days in office Theodore Roosevelt was either hated or admired. An ardent admirer once exclaimed to him, "Mr. Roosevelt, you are a great man!" In characteristic honesty he replied, "No, Teddy Roosevelt is simply a plain, ordinary man—

highly motivated." It is safe to say that his answer describes most great leaders, including Nehemiah: plain and ordinary, yet *highly motivated*. Edwin Markham expressed similar admiration for Abraham Lincoln: "Here was a man to hold against the world, a man to match the mountains and the sea."[1]

It doesn't sound as if such lofty words could describe an ordinary person, does it? But wait a minute. When God puts His hand on a plain, ordinary person whom He has destined for leadership, that person is given mountain-matching abilities, whether he be a Roosevelt, a Lincoln, a Nehemiah—or a person like you or me. He motivates leaders to accomplish goals, to keep on working, to pass the bricks! Nehemiah, although an ordinary man underneath, emerges as one of the most significant leaders in history. He was highly motivated to do a job for God that involved many difficult circumstances.

Before we get into the exciting specifics of learning about effective leadership from Nehemiah, we need to get some quick history under our belts. Trying to study and appreciate Nehemiah without knowledge of this transitional period of history would be like visiting old Concord Bridge in Massachusetts or the Liberty Bell in Philadelphia with no knowledge of the Revolutionary War. So take a moment in the remaining pages of this chapter to catch a glimpse of what led up to the times in which Nehemiah lived. Then we will be ready for a careful study of Nehemiah the leader.

A Look at the Times

Jewish history begins with Abraham at approximately 2000 BC. But it was not until one thousand years later that Israel took on world significance as a nation under Saul, David, and Solomon. In the successive reigns of these three kings, Israel's flag flew proudly over the nation. Israel was finally recognized as a major military power under King David's forty-year command.

David expanded Israel's territory tenfold, defeated the nation's neighboring enemies, and ushered in an era of security and prosperity the Hebrew people would not see again until the latter half of the twentieth century. Upon his death, David turned his throne over to his son Solomon. And if you know your Bible, you know that by the last part of his life Solomon had compromised his integrity by allowing idol worship in Israel. Consequently, God judged him.

> So the Lord said to Solomon, "Because you have done this, and you have not kept My covenant and My statutes, which I have commanded you, I will surely tear the kingdom from you, and will give it to your servant." (1 Kings 11:11)

When Solomon died, there was a split in the nation's military ranks. Israel became a divided kingdom: Ten tribes migrated to the north and settled in Samaria; the other two went south and settled in Jerusalem and the surrounding areas. The northern tribes during this period of division and civil war were called Israel and the southern group, Judah (see chart 1 on page 18).

Just as the lowest ebb in American history was when its citizens took up arms against one another in the Civil War, so it was with this north-south split in Jewish history. They reached their darkest hour nationally not when they were attacked from without, but when they were divided within, when the walls of their spiritual heritage began to crumble. During this time of division, the leaders of both sides led their people into idolatry. Soon, chaos displaced the Law of Moses and neither side looked any different than the pagan nations surrounding them.

God judged Israel by allowing the Assyrians to invade and conquer in 722 BC. Those ten tribes were finished; the Northern Kingdom ceased to exist. But some of the people from the North fled to the South to escape Assyrian control.

The land of Judah remained a Jewish nation for more than three hundred years. However, in 586 BC, Babylon's King Nebuchadnezzar invaded Jerusalem (and all Judah) and took the people captive. This began the Babylonian Captivity. The biblical account in 2 Chronicles 36:18–19 records the end of Judah's history and the beginning of the Babylonian Captivity.

> All the articles of the house of God, great and small, and the treasures of the house of the Lord, and the treasures of the king and of his officers, he brought them all to Babylon. Then they burned the house of God and broke down the wall of Jerusalem, and burned all its fortified buildings with fire and destroyed all its valuable articles. (2 Chronicles 36:18–19)

They burned the house of God, the temple, and they broke down the protective wall around the city. (Take special note of the words "house of God" and "the wall," for we want to discuss what they mean a bit later.) All the fortified buildings were destroyed with fire, as were the valuable articles in the temple.

After the Babylonian takeover, Jerusalem was completely leveled. The magnificent place where God's glory was once displayed was destroyed. The wall lay in ruins, and wild dogs fed upon any edible remains. The armies of Babylon marched back home with all the treasures of Judah.

Psalm 137 was written during this dismal time. The psalmist cried out, "How can we sing the Lord's song in a foreign land?" (v. 4). Babylon had come and taken away the Israeli captives. Their song was ended. 2 Chronicles 36:20 adds a final word:

> Those who had escaped from the sword he carried away to Babylon; and they were servants to him and to his sons until the rule of the kingdom of Persia. (2 Chronicles 36:20)

That's important. Those Jews who lived through this siege of Jerusalem were bound together, chained like slaves, and sent to Babylon, a trek of more than eight hundred miles. And under Nebuchadnezzar and his wicked son, the Jews lived as they had centuries before in Egypt, as slaves to a foreign power.

But God didn't forget them. He had a purpose and a plan. Notice how verse 20 concludes: ". . . until the rule of the kingdom of Persia." A king named Cyrus ruled Persia and another king, Darius, ruled the neighboring Medes. The two nations were allies, but because the Persian force was the larger of the two, the two countries were often called simply "the kingdom of Persia." The Medes and the Persians invaded Babylon and overthrew it, forcing the Babylonian empire to surrender. 2 Chronicles 36:22 tells us:

> Now in the first year of Cyrus king of Persia—in order to fulfill the word of the Lord by the mouth of Jeremiah—the Lord

stirred up the spirit of Cyrus king of Persia, so that he sent a proclamation throughout his kingdom. (2 Chronicles 36:22)

Cyrus was not a believer, though on the surface he sounded like one. He was, nevertheless, concerned for the welfare of the Jews. God is not limited to working with His people only. He works in the lives and minds of unbelievers whenever He chooses. He moves the hearts of kings from one plan to another. And this is what He did with Cyrus. God's ultimate plan was to get the Jews back into their land.

Cyrus king of Persia . . . sent a proclamation throughout his kingdom, and also put it in writing, saying, "Thus says Cyrus king of Persia, 'The Lord, the God of heaven, has given me all the kingdoms of the earth, and He has appointed me to build Him a house in Jerusalem, which is in Judah. Whoever there is among you of all His people, may the Lord his God be with him, and let him go up!'" (2 Chronicles 36:22–23)

He said, in effect, "Let God's people go back—back to that city that was destroyed seventy years ago." Some Bible historians call this period of history "The Second Exodus." And so the Jews went back to Jerusalem under the leadership of three men.

"Company A" left first with Zerubbabel as its commanding officer. About eighty years later, another group, "Company B," left Babylon with Ezra as commander-in-chief. By this time, Cyrus had died and Artaxerxes took control of the Media-Persian Empire. Then, thirteen years later, Nehemiah led "Company C" back to Jerusalem—a city barely able to maintain security and order.

Remember I asked you to take special note of the terms "the house of God" and "the wall"? Here's why. "The house of God" is the primary subject of the Book of Ezra, while the Book of Nehemiah tells the story of "the wall" around Jerusalem. The Book of Ezra (which comes just before Nehemiah in the Old Testament), records how the house of God was rebuilt in the city of Jerusalem. But the temple was without protection for ninety years until God led Nehemiah to provide the leadership necessary to build a wall, and it is his account of that project that we call the Book of Nehemiah.

A Preview of the Book

Nehemiah 1:3 introduces the problem right away: "The remnant there in the province who survived the captivity are in great distress and reproach, and the wall of Jerusalem is broken down and its gates are burned with fire." Nehemiah responded: "When I heard these words, I sat down and wept and mourned for days; and I was fasting and praying before the God of heaven" (Nehemiah 1:4).

As the story of Nehemiah unfolds, we see the man who led his people in three successive roles. Early in the book, he serves as the *cupbearer* to the king. Midway through the story, he is the *builder* of the wall. In the third part of the book, he becomes the *governor* of the city and surrounding sections of Jerusalem (see chart 2 on page 19).

The Cupbearer

Nehemiah served King Artaxerxes as a cupbearer, which doesn't sound very impressive. The position sounds comparable to the dishwasher, or at best to the butler or the table waiter. But the cupbearer was far more important than that. The cupbearer tasted the wine before the king drank it, and he sampled the food before the king ate it. If somebody was trying to poison the king, no more cupbearer, but long live the king. Consequently, a high degree of trust would often develop between the taster and the partaker, between the cupbearer and the king. In fact, it has been suggested by historians that the cupbearer typically wielded great political influence, even more than the king's own family.

One Old Testament scholar mentions that the cupbearer "was often chosen for his personal beauty and attractions, and in ancient oriental courts was always a person of rank and importance. From the confidential nature of his duties and his frequent access to the royal presence, he possessed great influence."[2] Many cupbearers used their office to make a few extra bucks by putting in a good word for guys in the field who wanted a governmental promotion or VIP treatment. The cupbearer was an intimate counsel to the king.

Nehemiah had established a good relationship with King Artaxerxes, but he had a burden on his heart. He needed a political favor himself! When he heard there was a wall broken down in Jerusalem, Nehemiah heard God saying to him, "I want you to be the leader in the building of that wall. You are My man for the job."

But rather than racing into the king's presence and saying, "God told me to go back to Jerusalem to build a wall. I'm God's man!" Nehemiah prayed for guidance. In fact, all through the book you will find Nehemiah asking the Lord for direction.

The Builder

Beginning in chapter 2, verse 11, we see Nehemiah change to his second hat; he becomes a builder, and a wise one at that.

New ideas seem to go through three channels. First, rejection. You have an idea for something new. The person you tell it to says, "It won't work." You ask, "Why?" He replies, "Because we've tried it before." Or, "No one's ever done that before." It's rejected. The second channel is toleration: "Well, I'll allow it, as long as . . ." The third channel, the ideal response, is acceptance: "Let's go!"

Nehemiah, knowing the time was not right, didn't tell anybody that he was going to rebuild Jerusalem's wall. He got on his horse late at night (you can just see the moon shining on the ruins of the wall). Refer to the map on page 18 as you read the following:

> So I went out at night by the Valley Gate in the direction of the
> Dragon's Well and on to the Refuse Gate, inspecting the walls of
> Jerusalem which were broken down and its gates which were
> consumed by fire. Then I passed on to the Fountain Gate and
> the King's Pool, but there was no place for my mount to pass.
> (Nehemiah 2:13–14)

Apparently the rubble was piled so high he couldn't get by on his horse. But he saw enough to know what had to be done—and to know how difficult the job would be. But he kept his plans to himself.

> The officials did not know where I had gone or what I had done;
> nor had I as yet told the Jews, the priests, the nobles, the officials
> or the rest who did the work. (Nehemiah 2:16)

Chapters 3, 4, and 5 of the Book of Nehemiah tell us about the work of building the wall. In spite of great odds and internal and external enemies, they finished the job. The climax, the "ribbon-cutting," comes in Nehemiah 6:15: "So the wall was completed on the twenty-fifth of the month Elul, in fifty-two days."

The Governor

Finally, Nehemiah changed hats again. He became the governor. The account of his election is in chapter 5, but we don't read of delegation of authority until chapter 7:

> Now when the wall was rebuilt and I had set up the doors, and the gatekeepers and the singers and the Levites were appointed, then I put Hanani my brother, and Hananiah the commander of the fortress, in charge of Jerusalem, for he was a faithful man and feared God more than many. (Nehemiah 7:1–2)

Nehemiah was a clear-thinking leader; he saw the importance of spiritual men at the helm of the city. Nehemiah also made a long list of the families in Jerusalem, starting with those who had returned first. They became the charter members of his new walled community.

Looking ahead to chapter 8, verse 9, we read:

> Then Nehemiah, who was the governor, and Ezra the priest and scribe, and the Levites who taught the people said to all the people, "This day is holy to the Lord your God; do not mourn or weep." For all the people were weeping when they heard the words of the law. (Nehemiah 8:9)

Let's pause here and summarize. Nehemiah came into the city

and rebuilt the wall. In chapter 8, we read that the people stood in a great court and asked that the book of the Law of Moses be brought out. From a wooden pulpit, Ezra read aloud to all the people. The people stood listening from early morning to midday and praised the name of their God.

You see, these people had been in captivity. They had been born to people in captivity. They had known spiritual desolation. And for the first time they saw their city showing signs of beginning anew. What an emotional moment it must have been when Ezra said, "Let's all stand and hear the Word of God." As he unrolled it and read from it, the people wept.

Nehemiah was the master bricklayer and general contractor! He changed from cupbearer to builder. When the wall was completed despite the harassment of enemies, he established a strong administration after his official promotion to the position of governor. His first action was to appoint godly men who would remind the people to purify themselves from sin and to praise God.

THE WALLS OF OUR LIVES

As we turn to look in detail at the characteristics of Nehemiah's leadership, consider a passage from Isaiah:

> Can a woman forget her nursing child
> And have no compassion on the son of her womb?
> Even these may forget, but I will not forget you.
> Behold, I have inscribed you on the palms of My hands;
> Your walls are continually before Me. (Isaiah 49:15–16)

God was saying to His people, "Your lives are like walls, continually before me. I have inscribed your life on my hands." What the walls were to Jerusalem, our lives are before God.

Quite frankly, I think the walls of our lives often lie in ruins through neglect. The leader who brings us to rebuild the walls is the Holy Spirit, and it is He who continues the work of reconstruction inside us. He tries His best to bring to our attention the condition of our walls, but sometimes we don't hear what He is saying. We are not hard of hearing; we simply don't listen.

Some of you are living within the walls of your life surrounded by ruin, and it all began very slowly. First there was a loose piece of stone or mortar. Then there was a crack that appeared in the wall. And then it broke into pieces, and there was a hole. Because of further neglect, the weeds of carnality began to grow through the wall. By and by, the enemy gained free access to your life.

You may be known as a solid Christian man or woman. But you know in your heart that although you are a Christian in the same sense that Jerusalem belonged to the Jews, the wall around your spiritual life that protects and defends you is in shambles. Such things as selfishness, lack of discipline, procrastination, immorality, not making time for God, compromise, and rebellion have come and sowed their ugly seeds. And they have begun to bear poisonous fruit.

Take serious inventory of your true condition. Before his project was ever undertaken, Nehemiah was informed and concerned. The first phase was *evaluation*. I sense in our day, among a number of people in the ranks of our evangelical family, a shallow frivolity concerning God. We tend to take Him lightly, as if He is our great big buddy. Then we hide behind the rationalization that "Nobody is perfect."

"After all," we tell ourselves, "I'm better than so-and-so and certainly better than I used to be." There's sort of a shrug of the shoulders and a mental rationalization: "Well, He'll understand." If this is your attitude, the enemy is living in your camp. Your walls are down.

Nehemiah's concern led him to the second phase, *reconstruction*. He prayed for guidance and correction. Have you been too busy for prayer?

"Oh, I've never been so busy! In all my life I've never been so busy," you may say.

But how about time with God?

You say, "Well, there's just not enough time in the day."

Get up earlier! Set aside your lunch hour. Skip a television show. You cannot afford *not* to have time with God each day. It was said of Hudson Taylor that the sun never rose for forty years in China without God finding him on his knees in prayer for that great land. Reconstruction, frankly, is hard work.

Consistency is the need of the hour. But erosion is our constant battle. Little by little, bit by bit, the process is set in motion. No one suddenly becomes base. The process of moral decay begins when the first piece of mortar comes loose and one stone drops to the side, which you let lie. Then another stone falls, and another.

Finally, Nehemiah honestly faced the situation and determined to stay with it until the task was done. The third phase was *perseverance*. You may be ready to weep over your sin. You may be at the place of confessing your wrongdoing, even to someone else. But you have not come to the place where, as we read in Nehemiah, "the people had a mind to work." They determined to hang in there.

That leathery, old saint, A. W. Tozer, put it so well:

Every farmer knows the hunger of the wilderness, that hunger which no modern farm machinery, no improved agricultural methods, can ever quite destroy. No matter how well prepared the soil, how well kept the fences, how carefully painted the buildings, let the owner neglect for a while his prized and valued acres and they will revert again to the wild and be swallowed up by the jungle or the wasteland. The bias of nature is toward the wilderness, never toward the fruitful field.[3]

The neglected heart, the life with crumbled walls, will soon be overrun by the world and chaos will prevail. Don't just repent. Rebuild! Persevere! Never give up!

I'm deeply concerned that you will read on, packing in theoretical facts on leadership, and continue to live without walls. If your heart has grown cold toward Christ and His church, deal with the problem now. Then as you read, expect the Holy Spirit to use the faith and persistence of Nehemiah to form within your heart a thirst and willingness to be the kind of leader that is blessed by God.

Chart 1

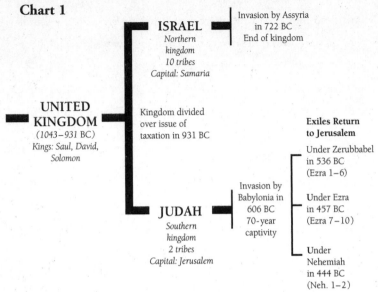

ISRAEL
*Northern
kingdom
10 tribes
Capital: Samaria*

Invasion by Assyria
in 722 BC
End of kingdom

**UNITED
KINGDOM**
*(1043–931 BC)
Kings: Saul, David,
Solomon*

Kingdom divided
over issue of
taxation in 931 BC

JUDAH
*Southern
kingdom
2 tribes
Capital: Jerusalem*

Invasion by
Babylonia in
606 BC
70-year
captivity

**Exiles Return
to Jerusalem**

Under Zerubbabel
in 536 BC
(Ezra 1–6)

Under Ezra
in 457 BC
(Ezra 7–10)

Under
Nehemiah
in 444 BC
(Neh. 1–2)

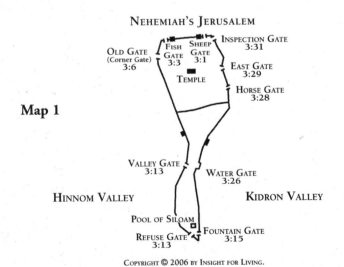

NEHEMIAH'S JERUSALEM

OLD GATE
(Corner Gate)
3:6

FISH
GATE
3:3

SHEEP
GATE
3:1

INSPECTION GATE
3:31

EAST GATE
3:29

TEMPLE

HORSE GATE
3:28

VALLEY GATE
3:13

WATER GATE
3:26

Map 1

HINNOM VALLEY

KIDRON VALLEY

POOL OF SILOAM

REFUSE GATE
3:13

FOUNTAIN GATE
3:15

NEHEMIAH

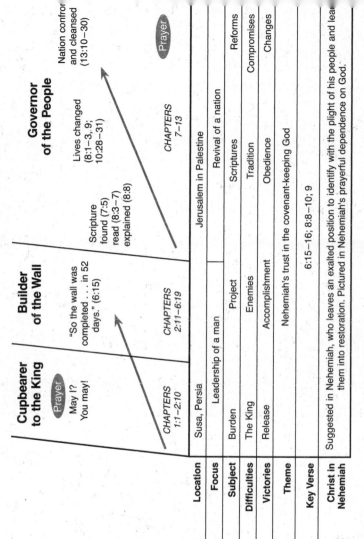

	Cupbearer to the King	Builder of the Wall	Governor of the People	
	Prayer May I? You may!	"So the wall was completed . . . in 52 days." (6:15)	Scripture found (7:5) read (8:3–7) explained (8:8)	Lives changed (8:1–3, 9; 10:28–31) Nation confront and cleansed (13:10–30) *Prayer*
	CHAPTERS 1:1–2:10	CHAPTERS 2:11–6:19	CHAPTERS 7–13	
Location	Susa, Persia		Jerusalem in Palestine	
Focus	Leadership of a man		Revival of a nation	
Subject	Burden	Project	Scriptures	Reforms
Difficulties	The King	Enemies	Tradition	Compromises
Victories	Release	Accomplishment	Obedience	Changes
Theme	Nehemiah's trust in the covenant-keeping God			
Key Verse	6:15–16; 8:8–10; 9			
Christ in Nehemiah	Suggested in Nehemiah, who leaves an exalted position to identify with the plight of his people and lea them into restoration. Pictured in Nehemiah's prayerful dependence on God.			

Two

A Leader—From the Knees Up!

Like most people in leadership positions, Nehemiah continually faced impossible circumstances. You will remember that he was eight hundred miles from what weighed heavily on his heart: his people who lived in the midst of the destruction in Jerusalem. To work fifteen or twenty miles from home is one thing, but Nehemiah was faced with a sixteen-hundred-mile round trip! We routinely travel at speeds up to seventy miles per hour. He would have considered it great progress to cover that much ground in two days.

To further complicate matters, Nehemiah answered to an unbeliever—King Artaxerxes. Before Nehemiah could leave his responsible post and go to Jerusalem to build the wall, something had to happen in the heart of Artaxerxes. His mind needed changing. When Nehemiah received God's orders, he did not rush into the king's oval office and give him the mandate, "Three years' leave of absence or I quit!" Instead, he went before God in prayer and trusted Him to open the doors and change the heart of his boss.

Here is how the story opens:

> The words of Nehemiah the son of Hacaliah. Now it happened
> in the month Chislev, in the twentieth year, while I was in Susa
> the capitol, that Hanani, one of my brothers, and some men
> from Judah came; and I asked them concerning the Jews who
> had escaped and had survived the captivity, and about Jerusalem.
> They said to me, "The remnant there in the province who sur-
> vived the captivity are in great distress and reproach, and the wall
> of Jerusalem is broken down and its gates are burned with fire."
> When I heard these words, I sat down and wept and mourned
> for days; and I was fasting and praying before the God of heaven.
> (Nehemiah 1:1–4)

Most likely, Nehemiah wrote his book himself. He described
himself simply as the son of Hacaliah, a man whose name does not
appear elsewhere in Scripture. Nehemiah gave his occupation in
verse 11 of the opening chapter: "I was the cupbearer to the king."
That is all we know about his earthly credentials. He was the cupbearer to the king, and he was the son of Hacaliah.

A Cupbearer with a Heart for God

As we noted in the previous chapter, being a cupbearer meant he was
the wine and food taster. He served as the screen between the public
and the king. It was a powerful position of intimacy and trust.

The story opens in the winter. It was the month of Chislev, or
December, in the twentieth year of the king. Looking back, we know

the year was about 445–444 BC, and the place is given to us in verse 1:
Nehemiah lived in Susa, the capital of the Media-Persian empire, the
Washington DC of the day. Even more significantly, Susa was recognized by the Jews as the capital of the then-known world. It was a hub
of activity, the place of ultimate decision-making; late-breaking news of
the empire often came to the attention of King Artaxerxes through the
lips of his cupbearer. Nehemiah was the king's right-hand man.

In verse 2, Hanani, one of Nehemiah's brothers (I take this to
mean one of his blood brothers) and some men from Judah arrived.
Nehemiah's two concerns were the Jews who escaped and Jerusalem.

It has been said that the true Jew never completely forgets
Jerusalem. This was certainly true of Nehemiah. He wanted to know
about the people; he wanted to know the condition of the beloved
city. Those returning from Judah told him, " . . . The remnant there
in the province who survived the captivity are in great distress and
reproach . . ." (Nehemiah 1:3)

The Hebrew word translated as *great distress* means "misery" and
"calamity." The people who were in that city were in a vulnerable
position. In fact, the men added, they were under reproach, using a
term meaning "disgrace, contempt, or scorn." It's closely related to a
term in other Semitic languages that means "sharp, cutting, penetrating, or piercing." The picture painted by this term portrays someone
suffering the lacerations of cutting words. The Jews were severely
criticized and slandered by people who were enemies of the faith.

Nehemiah was brokenhearted. Verses 4 through 11 contain his
reaction, and it is here we see his gift of leadership begin to emerge.
I am deeply impressed with the fact that, though he possessed a high-
ranking position in the world, he had a heart that was very tender

toward God. It is rare to find these combined strengths in a person: high position in the eyes of the world with genuine tenderness before God.

Perhaps you are in a position of great importance. It's a vulnerable place in which to live. Each promotion endangers your spiritual life just a little more than before, and your position threatens your walk with God. It doesn't have to cripple your walk, but it can be damaging, and often is. Scripture is replete with examples of people who were promoted from one level to the next and suffered from "promotion erosion"—pride slowly but surely overtook them. I deal with this problem at length in Chapter 8.

MARKS OF A COMPETENT LEADER

Nehemiah, touched by the need of his people, "sat down and wept and mourned" and "was fasting and praying before the God of heaven" (Nehemiah 1:4). In verses 4 through 11, I find four very significant factors that characterize the lives of competent, spiritual leaders. I want you to remember them, so I will list them as they occurred in Nehemiah's experience. Let's take them in order.

1. *A leader has a clear recognition of the needs.* The beginning of verse 4 reads, "When I heard these words . . ." Nehemiah wasn't preoccupied; he didn't live in a dream world, isolated from reality. He asked, "What's the condition?" They replied, "It's a miserable situation." He heard what they said. You may think recognizing needs is an elementary concept, especially for leaders. But I have met many people in responsible leadership positions who never seem to see the problems they ought to be solving.

I remember taking a course in seminary under a brilliant Bible teacher. In fact, he was known all over the world for his knowledge of Scripture. But he was so well read and had known the answers for so long that he had forgotten there could be any questions! We would raise our hands and pose a problem, and he would blink and say, "Problem? What problem?"

There is a very simple reason for this "no problem" mentality: preoccupation. Have you ever been around a preoccupied professor or boss? Some of you live with a preoccupied spouse, and you know getting his or her attention is no easy task.

"Honey, I want to talk with you about something that's happened."

"Uh-huh."

"It's leaking . . . in the other room . . . it's running out onto the floor."

"Uh-huh."

It's remarkable how individuals who have a high level of responsibility often have difficulty relating at the problem level.

I have a friend who is quite successful in the construction business. In fact, he is a prominent builder in his city. But he hates reality. As a result, his family has suffered. He has been deceived, ripped off, and misused time and again because he hates to face issues and refrains from asking hard, follow-up questions. He is creative, visionary, warm, loving, and very tender toward the things of God. But he just doesn't *see* the problems. He avoids confrontation by saying, "Don't tell me the problems; let's talk about the good things."

Now I think a person can be so problem-oriented that problems are all he can think about—and that's not good either. But the person who is a real leader has a clear recognition of needs.

Are you aware of needs? How about the needs in your own family? Are you sensitive as a parent or as a mate? Maybe you live alone. Do you know what is on your parents' hearts, where the scales tip? If you teach, do you know your students' needs—the kids who fill your classroom? If you are in business leadership, are you in touch with more than the perquisites of executive privilege? What about those otherwise hidden areas where problems start and fester?

2. *A leader is personally concerned with the needs.* Nehemiah went a step beyond recognition of the problem. He not only heard these matters, but he sat down and identified with them.

Alan Redpath once wrote:

Let us learn this lesson from Nehemiah: you never lighten the load unless first you have felt the pressure in your own soul. You are never used of God to bring blessing until God has opened your eyes and made you see things as they are.[1]

Nehemiah was called to build the wall, but first he wept over the ruins: "The walls are down. Oh, God! How can these walls remain down and these people continue in safety?" But the normal response is, "Oh, the walls are down! Who fouled up? Who blew it?" Or, "They've been back there all these years and nobody has built those walls? Send me their names; I'll deal with them." Instead of looking for someone to blame, Nehemiah empathized and reacted with compassion.

Before I go any further, I want us to learn a very practical lesson about a father who refused to recognize a specific family need. The story is found in 1 Samuel 3. All through my childhood, I remember being told in Sunday school about young Samuel who was asleep on his cot when somebody said, "Samuel! Samuel!" And he ran over to Eli and said, "What is it?" And Eli said, "Go back to sleep. It was not I." Again, the voice woke Samuel, and the same thing happened. Finally, Eli said, "Listen, that's God you're hearing." And the story always ended there. I wondered, "Why in the world did God wake him so often? What was the Lord trying to tell him?" Later I found the answer in verses 11 and 12:

> The Lord said to Samuel, "Behold, I am about to do a thing in Israel at which both ears of everyone who hears it will tingle. In that day I will carry out against Eli all that I have spoken concerning his house, from beginning to end." (1 Samuel 3:11–12)

Don't tell me God isn't concerned about a leader's home. Here was Eli, a spiritual leader in Israel, and God's concern was over his home. Read verse 13:

> For I have told him that I am about to judge his house forever for the iniquity which he knew, because his sons brought a curse on themselves and he did not rebuke them. (1 Samuel 3:13)

Underline in your Bible "he knew" and "he did not rebuke them." Are there times when you know something wrong is going on at your house, but you refuse to be involved in correcting it? We carelessly pull the shades on reason and say, "Well, somehow it's going to work out."

God has appointed the father to one of the most difficult leadership positions in all the world: to lead his home. He motivates, sets the pace, gives guidance and encouragement, and handles discipline. Eli knew all this, but he would not rebuke his sons when they disobeyed God. Maybe he figured the leaders at the temple would straighten out the kids. It's tragic how many people leave the job of child rearing to the church, causing the church to live under the constant indictment, "The worst kids in the world are the church kids." The church gets the blame. But it's not a church problem; it's a home problem. The church can seldom resurrect what the home consistently puts to death.

As we turn back to Nehemiah as a model for leadership, realize that we are not talking only about Nehemiah and some ancient city at the dawn of history. We are talking about *today*. The higher you are elevated in what the world calls success, the easier it is to fade into theoretical preoccupation and to leave the realistic "lesser things" to work themselves out.

Notice, in verse 4, that Nehemiah was "fasting and praying." What does it mean to fast? It means to miss a meal for one major purpose: zeroing in on your walk with God. Some people fast one day a week. Some people fast one day a month. Some never fast even though it is mentioned rather frequently in Scripture. When our motive is right, it is amazing what we can accomplish with the Lord when we occasionally save the time it would take to fix, eat, and clean up after a meal and instead invest it on our knees. The more responsibility we shoulder, the more time we need for contemplation before our Father.

3. *A serious leader goes first to God with the need.* In verse 5 we

hear Nehemiah say, "I beseech Thee, O Lord God of heaven." He prayed.

What is your first response when a need comes to your attention? I can tell you what it is because it's usually my first response in my own fallen human nature: "How can I work this out?" or "What did so-and-so do wrong to make that happen?"

Your people problem, whatever it may be, will not be completely solved until you take it to God in prayer. I mentioned this in the first chapter, and it is illustrated in Nehemiah's life. Someday you will look back at the rational decisions you made in the flesh, and you will hate the day you acted upon them. Prayer, I repeat, is absolutely essential in the life of a leader.

Look at how Nehemiah behaved before the Lord. First, he *praised God.*

> I beseech You, O Lord God of heaven, the great and awesome God, who preserves the covenant and lovingkindness for those who love Him and keep His commandments. (Nehemiah 1:5)

He knew he was not coming to just another man, but rather to the God of heaven.

For whom did Nehemiah work? The king. Was this king great and mighty on the earth? The mightiest! But compared to God, King Artaxerxes was nothing. And so it stands to reason that when we go to God in prayer, we put things into proper perspective. If you are having difficulty loving or relating to an individual, take him to God. Bother the Lord with this person. Don't you be bothered with him—leave him at the throne.

Next, in verses 6 and 7, he *confessed his part in the problem.*

Let Your ear now be attentive and Your eyes open to hear the
prayer of Your servant which I am praying before You now, day
and night, on behalf of the sons of Israel Your servants, confessing the sins of the sons of Israel which we have sinned against
You; I and my father's house have sinned. We have acted very
corruptly against You . . . (Nehemiah 1:6–7)

Notice the words "we" and "I." The confession was not on behalf
of someone else's failure. The confession had to do with Nehemiah's
part in the problem. What do we do when we are in conflict with
another person? We initially blame the other person (our fallen state
coming through again). We usually think of six or seven ways the
other person has manifested his stubbornness and unwillingness to
change, but we seldom consider our part in the problem. But it
works both ways. So the very first thing Nehemiah said in regard to
the problem was, "Lord, I am culpable. I am not only wanting to be
part of the answer, I am confessing myself to be part of the problem."

There may be husband-wife difficulties at your house or strained
pupil-teacher relationships at school. There may be strife between a
parent and child. And invariably, you will think of your mate or your
child or your mom or your teacher or your pupil as being the problem, which is not necessarily so, or at least not entirely.

I plead with you—as you go before God in prayer concerning
any unresolved personal conflicts, take the attitude reflected in these
words: "Lord, I bring before you these areas where I have caused an
irritation. This is my realm of responsibility. I can't change this other

person. But God, I can tell you that this is my part in it; forgive me."

Nehemiah didn't stop with confession. Next, he *claimed the promise*. When he went to God in prayer, he praised the Father, confessed his part in the wrong, and claimed the promise God had given.

Verse 8 reads, "Remember the word which You commanded Your servant Moses . . ." What was Nehemiah doing? He was quoting a verse of Scripture to God. He quoted not only from Leviticus 26 but also from Deuteronomy 30. He knew the Book. "Lord, I open the Book before You. I bring You the very words You spoke, the promise You made. And I'm claiming it, Lord, right now."

What was the promise? It was twofold. The promise was that if the people of Israel disobeyed, they would go into a foreign land. That had come to pass. The second part was that when that time of captivity was ended, God would bring the Jews back to Jerusalem and protect them. That part was unfulfilled. So Nehemiah was saying, "Lord, the first part is true. We've disobeyed and we've been in captivity. But, Lord, You made a promise to bring us back into the city and protect us, and that has not yet come to pass. I am claiming that it will."

The apostle Paul wrote:

Yet, with respect to the promise of God, he did not waver in unbelief but grew strong in faith, giving glory to God, and being fully assured that what God had promised, He was able also to perform. (Romans 4:20–21)

God does not lightly give out promises. He says, "I promise you that if you will give Me your burden, I will bear it. If you will seek first My kingdom, I will add all these other things to you. If you will make your heart right before Me, I will lead you into a path of stability and prosperity."

That doesn't mean He will fill your wallet. It does mean He will give you peace, in a way the world is not able to know: "I will promote you to a place of My level of significance, and you will be greatly satisfied."

Nehemiah said, "Lord, You promised that Your people will be protected in that city, and I'm claiming it right now."

Finally Nehemiah *brought his petition or desire before God.* His petition was a bold one.

> O Lord, I beseech You, may Your ear be attentive to the prayer of Your servant and the prayer of Your servants who delight to revere Your name, and make Your servant successful today and grant him compassion before this man. (Nehemiah 1:11)

Have you ever prayed this? "Lord, make me successful. Make me find that place in the center of Your will where heavenly prosperity rests, in whatever level it may be. May I reach the maximum so that I am, in Your eyes, prosperous. And, Lord, grant me favor with those in authority over me!" That's bold petitioning.

4. *A leader is available to meet the need himself.* "Make me successful. Grant me compassion in his eyes." Nehemiah recognized the need clearly. He got *involved* in it. He *took it to God.* Now he was *available* to meet the need, if that was what God desired.

A genuine leader is marked by diligent faithfulness in the midst of a task. And that faithfulness is more than passive inclination. It is demonstrated by being available and personally involved in meeting needs. There is not much benefit in leadership by proxy.

During my days in the Marine Corps we were often told that an officer stays with his company and a squad leader stays with his squad. As the intensity of the battle increases, the more his presence means. Those in command were instructed to be available, to get involved. Continued aloofness among military leaders weakens the morale of those under their command.

Leaders in God's work would do well to remember that principle. Prayer is primary—but not theoretical prayer. Prayer that gets the job done includes the conviction, "I'm available, Lord—ready and willing."

Benefits of Prayer

Nehemiah 1 is a blend of prayer and action. All who lead must place a high priority on prayer. Why is prayer so important? Here are the four shortest reasons I know.

Prayer *makes me wait*. I cannot pray and work at the same time. I have to wait to act until I finish praying. Prayer forces me to leave the situation with God; it makes me wait.

Secondly, prayer *clears my vision*. Southern California often has an overhanging weather problem in the mornings, because of its coastal location, until the sun "burns through" the morning fog. Prayer does that. When you first face a situation, is it foggy? Prayer will "burn through." Your vision will clear so you can see through God's eyes.

Thirdly, prayer *quiets my heart*. I find that prayer is the best channel for removing my worries. When I turn my anxiety into prayer, my spirit grows quiet. Prayer replaces angst with peace. Knees don't knock when we kneel on them!

Fourthly, prayer *activates my faith*. After praying I am more prone to trust God. And how petty and negative and critical I am when I don't pray! Prayer sets faith on fire.

Don't just fill the margins in your Bible with words and thoughts about ways a leader prays. Do it! Don't stop with just a sterile theology of prayer. Pray! Prayer was the first major step Nehemiah took in his journey to effective leadership.

> Got any rivers you think are uncrossable?
> Got any mountains you cannot tunnel through?
> God specializes in things thought impossible;
> He does the things others cannot do.[2]

The Lord is the Specialist we need for these "uncrossable" and impossible experiences. He delights in accomplishing what we cannot pull off. But He awaits our cry. He listens for our request. Nehemiah was quick to call for help. His favorite position when faced with problems was the kneeling position.

How about you?

THREE

Preparation for a Tough Job

There are few areas of life in which we live or work that do not come ready-equipped with a superior—a boss or other authority figure. Student, teacher, nurse, executive, salesman, airline pilot, coach, chef, or scientist all have immediate superiors whose presence significantly controls and affects their lives. It is our task to develop qualities of leadership germinating within ourselves while still being accountable to these superiors in our individual spheres of influence. That isn't easy! Leaders are usually better at leading than being led.

The question remains: *When that time of confrontation comes—* between boss and employee, parent and child, coach and player, teacher and pupil—*how do we handle it?* That question becomes increasingly complex when the superior is insensitive to or unconcerned with spiritual things.

Hudson Taylor once said, "It is possible to move men through God by prayer alone." As a leader, you will come to places where those in authority over you are beyond your power to change. The message God has for you at that point is prayer.

Proverbs 21 is an interesting proverb for a couple of reasons. First, it is a comparative proverb in which something is likened to something else. Most comparative proverbs end with the comparison and leave it at that. But this proverb comes to a conclusion in what could be called the declarative part of the proverb. It concludes with a timeless principle, but let's first consider the comparison.

A PROVERB WITH A PUNCH

"The king's heart is like channels of water in the hand of the Lord." The sentence in Hebrew does not begin with "The king's heart . . ." but with the word "channels," referring to small irrigation ditches that run from a main reservoir to dry, thirsty flatlands that need to be filled with water. "Like irrigation canals carrying water is the heart of the king in Yahweh's hand," the original says. But what does this proverb tell us about our superiors? The writer was saying that the heart that communicates decisions and attitudes is in the Lord's hand. That is, God is sovereign.

Now look at the last part of the first verse, the declaration: "He [Yahweh] turns it wherever He wishes."

The Lord has in His hand the heart of a king. (Whether the king is a believer or not is unimportant.) Because the Lord has the king's heart in His hand, He literally "causes it to be bent" wherever He is pleased. So putting it all together, the verse could read, "Like irrigation canals carrying water, so is the heart of the king in Yahweh's hand. He causes it to bend and incline in whatever direction He pleases."

What is true of the king is true of your superior! To understand your boss, you must become acquainted with God's method of operation, for the Lord has the heart of your superior in His hand. Pause momentarily and rivet that thought in your mind.

A Boss Who Won't Budge

We will see how the story of Nehemiah beautifully illustrates the truth revealed in Proverbs 21:1. Nehemiah worked under a man who just happened to be the king of Persia. There's a saying that goes, "Don't try to change it. It's like the law of the Medes and the Persians," and it means that something is impossible to change! Artaxerxes, king of the Medes and the Persians, had a reputation for being impossible to change. Nehemiah was in an influential position, for he played an intimate part in the king's life. But Nehemiah's heart was not in Persia; it was in Jerusalem. He wanted to go back to his beloved city and rebuild those walls, but he couldn't just leave his job. God had to work through the heart of the king.

Nehemiah sought the Lord in prayer because he knew that was the only way to change the king's heart. He prayed intently:

> O Lord, I beseech You, may Your ear be attentive to the prayer of Your servant and the prayer of Your servants who delight to revere Your name, and make Your servant successful today and grant him compassion before this man. (Nehemiah 1:11)

Now look at his request: "and make Your servant successful today and grant him compassion before this man." Nehemiah, cupbearer to the king, said in effect, "Lord, I ask You to change the heart of the king; alter his attitudes. Change the situation so that I may be allowed to do Your will with his pleasure—the pleasure of my superior." He didn't rashly run to Jerusalem, but he laid his problem before God.

WAITING IS ESSENTIAL

What happened after Nehemiah prayed to the Lord? Nothing! At least not right away. Nehemiah's story opened in the month of Chislev (see Nehemiah 1:1), and it resumes in the month of Nisan (Nehemiah 2:1).

Chislev is December; Nisan is April. For four months nothing happened.

Have you ever had that disillusioning experience? Perhaps you heard the preacher say one Sunday, "Just pray to God; give Him the situation." So you went home and prayed about a frustrating problem and ended with the favorite American prayer: "Lord, give me patience—and I want it NOW!" Then Monday morning came and nothing changed; what's worse, a *month* from then, nothing had changed. "Lord, are You awake? Did You hear me?" you ask. Another month passes, and then another. That was Nehemiah's experience.

The prayer warrior quickly learns the patience of waiting. And so Nehemiah was doing just that—waiting. In the diary he kept, nothing was entered for those four months because nothing happened. He waited. There was no visible glimmer of hope, no change. He kept waiting and trusting and counting on God to move the heart of his superior.

Now look at verse 1 of chapter 2:

And it came about in the month Nisan, in the twentieth year of King Artaxerxes, that wine was before him, and I took up the wine and gave it to the king. Now I had not been sad in his presence. (Nehemiah 2:1)

The Living Bible emphasizes the waiting period: "One day in April four months later."

Here Nehemiah was in a familiar situation. The king and his queen were reclining together, having finished their sumptuous meal. The delightful aroma of the food permeated the room. Nehemiah poured them some of their favorite vintage and brought it to them. "I took up the wine and gave it to the king," Nehemiah said, adding an insightful statement: "Now I had not been sad in his presence." Do you know how to tell when someone wants you to know he has been spending long hours in prayer? Look at him. If he wants to show you how very spiritual he is, he wears his "super pious look," usually evidenced by a *long* face.

But Nehemiah didn't have that gloomy glare. For four months he did not show that face. Incredible, isn't it? If we were to spend three or four hours on our knees, we would get up with a face that tells everyone we've been praying earnestly about something. Nehemiah had left his concern with the Lord, saying, "Lord, take over. It's Your timing; I'm going to rest it with You." Consequently, he could honestly report, "I had not been sad in his [the king's] presence."

Four months, however, can seem a long time to wait for some sign of response from the Lord. Everybody's got a breaking point.

Nehemiah had come to the place where he had just begun to wonder, "Is it ever going to happen?" Maybe this was his blue Monday, for Nehemiah was rather sad when he served the royal couple that day.

> So the king said to me, "Why is your face sad though you are not sick? This is nothing but sadness of heart." Then I was very much afraid. (Nehemiah 2:2)

I appreciate Nehemiah's honesty. Many leaders no longer admit their human weaknesses. Not Nehemiah. He honestly said, "When the king said that to me, I got scared." No matter how great you may become, it is important you let the cracks in your life show. Rather than hiding them—admit them!

Nehemiah had good reason to be frightened. Subjects who were noticeably sad or melancholic in the presence of the king were usually killed for "raining on his parade." Keep Nehemiah's feelings in mind as you read verses 3 and 4:

> I said to the king, "Let the king live forever. Why should my face not be sad when the city, the place of my fathers' tombs, lies desolate and its gates have been consumed by fire?" Then the king said to me, "What would you request?" So I prayed to the God of heaven. (Nehemiah 2:3–4)

This was the moment Nehemiah had been awaiting! God opened the door. And Nehemiah instantly prayed, asking the Lord for wisdom in choosing words to express his desire to the king.

Have you ever been in the midst of answered prayer? You prayed and waited, prayed and waited, and finally the door swung open. For a brief moment you stood there almost unable to believe the reality of the answer. Your mind raced as you spontaneously sought God's leading: "O God, this is such a critical point. Help me to take these steps very carefully."

That's precisely where Nehemiah was at this juncture in the story. God had thrown the door wide open.

"What would you request?" Artaxerxes asked Nehemiah. The king's heart was in the hands of Yahweh. God had adjusted the thinking of King Artaxerxes so that he was receptive to his employee's wishes. "What do you want, Nehemiah? What's worth getting sad over?"

Nehemiah responded:

If it please the king, and if your servant has found favor before you, send me to Judah, to the city of my fathers' tombs, that I may rebuild it. (Nehemiah 2:5)

That's Nehemiah's answer, his request. He had sought the Lord's help to "change the heart of the king." He had patiently waited four long months for His answer. And now his petition was granted. He made known his desire.

Nehemiah bared his heart before his boss and waited for his response. It was not long in coming. Nehemiah wrote, "Then the king said to me, the queen sitting beside him . . ." (Nehemiah 2:6)

Now, why in the world, we ask ourselves, did Nehemiah take the trouble to point out the queen's presence? It really makes one wonder, doesn't it? In Hebrew, the word translated here as *queen* actually means "a close intimate friend, a contact, or a consort." Maybe the queen leaned over to her husband and whispered something. Maybe he first spoke with her, and she gave the king the nudge he needed. Whatever happened, the king asked, "How long will your journey be, and when will you return?" The last of verse 6 reads: "I gave him a definite time."

This tells me the king didn't want Nehemiah to stay away. He was doing a good job as cupbearer. Despite his concern for Jerusalem, Nehemiah's attitude at work was positive. He was a diligent worker. That, my friend, is a rare person! When your heart is somewhere else, it is really difficult to perform the task at hand. But for four months, Nehemiah had faithfully done his job and so the king didn't think, "Man, I've been looking for a way to get rid of him. Now's my chance. Go on to Jerusalem." Instead, he asked, "When will you come back?"

Look at Nehemiah's marvelous response: "I gave him a definite time." That's great! I weary of people who call it "faith" when they can't tell you their plans. Have you ever heard an individual say, "No, we're not going to think this through. We're just going by 'faith.' God will lead us." The calculating businessman says, "Uh-huh, yeah. You'll be back needing more cash before you're halfway there." The presence of faith does not mean an absence of organization.

GOD HONORS A PLAN

"I gave him a definite time."

Do you know that God honors order and organization? Can you imagine what had previously transpired in Nehemiah's mind in order for him to provide an immediate, on-the-spot answer? Nehemiah had a plan. You see, he had been doing more than praying for four months. He had been planning. That in itself was an exercise in faith.

He was so sure God would let him go that he even drew up an agenda in case the king asked him how much leave of absence he would need!

Proverbs 16:9 says, "The mind of man plans his way, but the Lord directs his steps." Going out by faith doesn't mean you're going out in a disorderly or haphazard manner. You think through a project and count the cost financially. (I deal with this issue at length in chapter 7.)

I am greatly concerned that so many people who undertake some project in the Lord's work enter without careful planning. They abruptly begin without thinking through questions such as, "Where will this lead us? How can I express this in clear, unmistakable, concrete terms? What are the costs, the objectives, the possible pitfalls? What process should be used?" I could name a number of individuals or families who entered the ministry with enthusiasm but later dropped out because they had not considered the cost. Some of the most disillusioned people I know are those in the Lord's work who are now paying the price of not thinking through their plans.

Admittedly, planning is hard work. Thinking isn't as exciting as involvement, but without it confusion is inevitable. Good leaders do their homework!

Some may read Nehemiah 2:7–9 and think Nehemiah presumptuous. No, he's practical. When King Artaxerxes said, "Fine. You may go," Nehemiah continued, "Now wait a minute, King, before I leave there are a couple of things I want to talk about." Notice the gracious way he starts his request:

> If it please the king, let letters be given me for the governors of
> the provinces beyond the River, that they may allow me to pass
> through until I come to Judah, and a letter to Asaph the keeper

of the king's forest, that he may give me timber to make beams for the gates of the fortress which is by the temple, for the wall of the city and for the house to which I will go. (Nehemiah 2:7–8)

What's he asking for? He's asking for timber to build himself a house. That's a practical mind at work. You see, during these four months of waiting, Nehemiah was planning. The old Revolutionary War soldiers used to say, "Trust in God, but keep your powder dry." Pray to God, but make your plans, set your sights, think through the obstacles. Many people in God's work are shortsighted. Imagine Nehemiah's conversation with the first official outside the province of Susa if he had not planned ahead.

"Where are you going?"

"Well, I was hoping by faith to go to Jerusalem."

"Okay, where are your letters?"

"I don't have any letters."

"Then go back and get them."

So he would have had to go back and start all over.

Nehemiah was unlike the majority of "faith workers." Can't you picture him as he rode out of Susa and approached the first official?

"Here's a letter from the king."

"Who wrote it?"

"Artaxerxes. See . . . right there."

"Oh, man! Go on through."

Next, he entered Asaph's territory. Asaph was probably a negative thinker and maybe a tightwad.

"What do you want?"

"I want some timber."

"Nope! Only by requisition."

"Artaxerxes requisitioned that I have all the timber I want."

I'm sure Asaph checked out that requisition!

That's an example of perfect planning. God honors that kind of thinking. In fact, it illustrates a principle that I have seen at work in my own ministry: Wise planning on my part gives the Lord *more* opportunity to accomplish His ends, never less. And if truth be told, whenever the best plan has been missed, it's usually because I failed to put prayerful preparation behind my actions.

King Artaxerxes' positive response is stated in verse 6: "So it pleased the king to send me." Artaxerxes chose to send him, for God was on Nehemiah's side. It was just a matter of time. So Artaxerxes said, "That's fine. You may go." But did he stop there? Verse 8 concludes with the sentence, "And the king granted them to me because the good hand of my God was on me." He granted the letters—official "tickets" to get Nehemiah through. For four months, in the solitude of his prayer closet, Nehemiah had faithfully bombarded the throne of God: "Lord, send me to Jerusalem. Change the heart of the king so that I can go. Give me the green light!" And so Nehemiah had no doubt about the reason for this turn in events.

When the Lord has His hand on His appointed leaders, it's like a strong current moving people to respond. The Lord's hand was upon Nehemiah—and off he went, excited as he could be.

A Long Journey

Look at him en route. Verse 9 begins: "Then I came to the governors of the provinces beyond the River." There they are, just as he had expected. Nehemiah gave them the *king's* letters. Not only did the king send letters, but he also provided for Nehemiah over and above anything he had requested: "Now the king had sent with me officers of the army and horsemen" (Nehemiah 2:9).

The king offered to do more than Nehemiah had ever expected. "I'll not only send letters. I'll not only send you the okay to use my timber. I'll dispatch a few horsemen and a few soldiers, and they can go right along with you to protect you on your way." The king's gracious response came because his heart was in Yahweh's hand. God bent it wherever He pleased.

Nehemiah was on the way toward his goal, but in verse 10 we learn he came face to face with tough characters, the same ones he will run across again and again throughout the project. Look at them.

> When Sanballat the Horonite and Tobiah the Ammonite official heard about it, it was very displeasing to them that someone had come to seek the welfare of the sons of Israel. (Nehemiah 2:10)

Nehemiah faced his first opposition. When you walk by faith, you will invariably collide with the "Sanballats" and the "Tobiahs." If you have attempted any project requiring volunteer labor, you have encountered people who never tire of quoting the many variations of Murphy's Law: "Something bad will happen; it won't work." Many men and women live by that principle. Their whole life is one big negative. They have a critical spirit that smothers them. Whenever a challenge comes their way, they respond, "It can't be done!" So when Sanballat and Tobiah heard about Nehemiah's coming, their immediate response was, "No way!" You see, in addition to their negative attitudes, they had business investments with the citizens of Jerusalem, and Nehemiah's plan was sure to hurt their pocketbooks. And they began to make plans to oppose God's arrangement.

When you walk by faith and seek to lead, you will encounter the hostility of people who walk by sight. They are rebuked by the life of faith. They are especially rebuked because they don't have your vision. Sanballat and Tobiah heard about Nehemiah's ambitious plans to rebuild the city walls, and they were disturbed. Experiencing criticism and opposition doesn't necessarily mean you are outside God's will. Rather, it may reinforce the fact that you are in the very center of His plan.

As we saw in chapter 1, it was here Nehemiah "changed hats." No longer the cupbearer, he was now the construction engineer—the chief foreman. "So I came to Jerusalem and was there three days" (2:11). What was Nehemiah doing? We don't know. But judging from Nehemiah's track record, he was probably surveying the project during the day and kneeling before God at night.

Four Principles on Preparation

Nehemiah was preparing for a tough job, but he had his head on straight. The account of his preparation reveals what I consider to be four timeless principles for getting started God's way.

1. *Changing hearts is God's specialty.* Do not—I repeat—do not try to change people to fit your specifications. Don't try to manipulate people, play games, plan schemes, trick or deceive them. Instead, tell God on them! You may have a spouse who is just plain ornery, and you were

told this very morning that he or she does not plan to change. Let God deal with your mate's stubbornness.

Perhaps you are working with someone who is unfair and unbending, just plain *unreal.* How are you going to work in this situation? You've tried every manipulative move in the world without success. Talk to God about him or her.

You may know people in business or at school who are impossible creatures! God says, "Let Me at them. I will change them in ways you never would believe possible. Now, I'm not going to do it according to *your* timetable. I'm going to do it in My time." So between now and then, just relax.

But in the meantime, don't look so spiritual! When your spouse looks at you and says, "What are you doing?", don't turn to him or her with your eyelids at half-mast and say with a syrupy-sweet tone, "I'm just praying for you, Honey, that God will change your life."

That's the worst kind of manipulation. Just relax; let God take care of it. Then when change comes, guess who gets all the glory?

2. *Praying and waiting go hand in hand.* You have never really prayed until you've learned to wait, and to wait with release. Abandon yourself—let God change the king's heart. This is tough; it cuts across the grain of our human nature. But stand firmly. Give up your own homemade solutions and run the risk of letting God take charge.

3. *Faith is not a synonym for disorder or a substitute for careful planning.* People of faith need orderly minds. Leaders like Nehemiah think through the problems they face. Although their circumstances may allow them to go only half a step now, you can be sure they have already thought through the next twelve. Why? Because faith breeds organization—they go together.

Many years ago I had the opportunity of working with business-men, and it was one of the best learning experiences I have ever had. For more than three years, I met regularly with a group of salesmen associated with a large corporation. During those encounters I learned to think a lot more like businessmen, and I learned to appreciate them.

Almost everything that is presented to businessmen is communi-cated in terms of practical facts. These facts form the foundation upon which further discussion is built. From these committed Christian businessmen, I learned that God honors orderly thinking. He isn't pleased when we expect Him to spare us the pain of failure when we haven't even considered the cost of success. Of course, He does not want us to fail in that to which He calls us, but He is pleased when we plan.

4. *Opposition is to be expected when God's will is carried out.* When a person knows he is following God's will, it is unusual if least one person doesn't oppose him. I have rarely known it to be otherwise.

Don't you love this guy Nehemiah? He meets us right where we live. When he faced financial needs, he asked the king for letters. When he was afraid, he said, "Lord, give me the words to say." He was a man of faith, yet he carefully balanced faith with realism. He didn't have to have a detailed game plan in his hands, but he thought through the possible difficulties. He was a man of indomitable courage. Think of how he left all that he knew in Susa, got on his mount and took off—on an eight-hundred-mile journey. What a great experience! Yet how threatening and how risky from a human viewpoint.

Nehemiah has displayed four prerequisite steps to be taken by those who would desire to discover and develop their leadership potential and skills. He:

1. realized his own limitations—only God can change a man's heart;

2. turned to God—praying and waiting;

3. organized a feasible plan of action—while waiting for the Lord to answer;

4. pressed on, despite vocal opposition, to execute the plan— once God opened the way.

A plan is primary; waiting for God to work is essential; but following through with people is where it's at. In the next chapter we will move into the phase where the rubber of leadership meets the road of reality—the whole issue of stimulating and motivating others to roll up their sleeves and get the job done.

FOUR

Getting off Dead Center

Studying Nehemiah's story is a little like listening to a concerto. Just as a musical concerto features a soloist, this literary concerto features Nehemiah. He was not the conductor; God was. The soloist, however, played his instrument with beautiful technique.

A concerto employs a major theme or melody. The main theme of the Book of Nehemiah is leadership. There are parallel themes such as planning, prayer, opposition, and motivation; but in spite of the secondary melodies, the basic theme of leadership comes through over and over again. And every concerto has at least three major movements. Often each one is played in contrast to the others. One may be quiet and soft; the next, passionate and stirring; and the last may have a touch of all the others, closing with a climactic crescendo.

The same is true in Nehemiah's story of leadership. The first movement takes place from chapter 1 through chapter 2, verse 10, and in it we see Nehemiah playing his part as the king's cupbearer.

Beginning at verse 11 of chapter 2 to the end of chapter 6, there is the soul-stirring second movement of Nehemiah as the builder. The final movement of the book commences when we reach chapter 7 and proceed—in one great crescendo—to the end of the book. In these last five chapters, we see Nehemiah as the governor.

If I could press the analogy just a bit further, I'd say that in no other movement does the soloist display greater technique or brilliance than in the second. When Nehemiah became a builder, determined to construct the wall around Jerusalem, I feel he became one of history's great leaders. However, his role as builder didn't begin very eloquently. The first movement ends after having built to a thundering climax in verse 11. You can almost hear the roll of the percussion, the blare of the horns, and the swelling harmony in the strings as Nehemiah proclaims, "I came to Jerusalem."

It is at this point that Nehemiah behaved quite differently from what we might expect. The hurried reader would think that Nehemiah, having reached his destination, would be driven by an inner burning compulsion to pull out the trowel, hire subcontractors, and hang the plumb line to get someone started on the wall—fast! But, he didn't do that. As a matter of fact, he didn't do anything. The concerto's second movement begins in the latter part of verse 11 with Nehemiah's statement, " . . . and [I] was there three days."

Why didn't he immediately go to work? Because he didn't know what God had for him. As a matter of fact, God was silent.

I don't know if it took place during those three days or right after them, but notice what happened next: "I arose in the night, I and a few men with me. I did not tell anyone . . ." (Nehemiah 2:12). In verse 16, Nehemiah reported further:

The officials did not know where I had gone or what I had done; nor had I as yet told the Jews, the priests, the nobles, the officials, or the rest who did the work. (Nehemiah 2:16)

It is this side of leadership that the uninvolved observer or even the workers never see. People have the false idea that a leader lives an exciting life in the limelight, basking in the experience of one ecstatic round of public applause after another. That image of a successful leader is promoted throughout the nation by exposure on television and in the press, or through internal communication channels within a company. But God begins this account of Nehemiah's second role by showing us that successful leaders know how to handle themselves in solitude.

Americans in particular feel an ache in our collective political veins to have leaders with this quality. Just when we thought we had recovered from the wounds of the Richard Nixon administration, Bill Clinton violated the public trust. Now I fear we will forever wonder what might be happening in the solitude of the Oval Office and that the days when we could trust our leaders' hidden actions are, tragically, behind us.

BEFORE ACTIVITY, MEANINGFUL SOLITUDE

If you think that being extremely busy equates itself with spirituality, learn a lesson from Nehemiah. It is not in the rush and the hurry of activity that a person gains the respect of those around him; it is what he does when he is all alone. Someone once aptly penned, "Character is what you are when nobody's looking."

What was happening during Nehemiah's silent days? Nehemiah

2:12 tells us, "I did not tell any one what my God was putting into my mind to do for Jerusalem." In that small, apparently insignificant phrase, there are volumes of knowledge. In the time of quietness when there was no activity, God was putting into Nehemiah's heart some top-priority information.

If you're a Sunday school teacher or pastor, you minister to others by teaching God's Word. But when alone, are you a student of the Word? Are you taking special note of what God has written?

Every once in a while a young man interested in being a pastor will ask me about the secret of a successful ministry, as if some clever behind-the-scenes maneuvering was involved. My answer is usually to the point: Do your homework. Be what you ought to be when nobody's looking. Do the job, and do it to the very best of your ability for the sheer joy of glorifying God in the process. And that requires time in the Scripture! That was a major secret of Nehemiah's success. He was faithful behind the scenes. He listened to the Lord.

While searching God's mind, Nehemiah received some objective direction.

> So I went out at night by the Valley Gate in the direction of the Dragon's Well and on to the Refuse Gate, inspecting the walls of Jerusalem which were broken down and its gates which were consumed by fire. Then I passed on to the Fountain Gate . . . (Nehemiah 2:13–14)

He went on down through the southern part of Jerusalem and back up the west side to the Fountain Gate. When Nehemiah came to the King's Pool, it was such a mess he couldn't even get by on his horse. He undoubtedly got off and walked along ahead of the mount. And he wrote: "[I] went up at night by the ravine and inspected the wall." Twice he talks about inspecting the damage (Nehemiah 2:13–15). The Hebrew word for *inspect* means "to look into something very carefully." It's a medical word for probing a wound to see the extent of the damage.

Nehemiah made a careful, conscious, probing examination of the wall for one reason: as leader, it was his job to be *aware* of the details and to develop a plan of action. But there is a vast difference between being aware of the details and being *lost* in those details. The individual who is able to stand back—being fully aware of the facts and yet not lost in them—is the one best equipped to lead. Nehemiah made a careful investigation of the facts. In his mind, he was developing a master plan for the whole process of construction and determining the necessary personnel and building materials.

As he inspected gates and walls and other sections of the city, he might have thought to himself: "Now, let's see. Who will be able to do this job best? That section will require a craftsman in this trade. Digging does not have to be done by skilled craftsmen. Pulling weeds and moving the old rubble—pushing it aside to make way—well, anyone can handle that."

In other words, Nehemiah planned it all out. He knew the job must fit the individual. All the groundwork for the gigantic undertaking was taking place in the silence and solitude of this time.

After Solitude, Strong Motivation

Nehemiah had done all his homework and made all his inspections. He was finally ready to discuss the need of rebuilding the city wall.

It was time to get the project moving. He hadn't said anything about his plans for three days. Then, when he had a good handle on the situation, he stood in front of the city council and said:

> You see the bad situation we are in, that Jerusalem is desolate and its gates burned by fire. Come, let us rebuild the wall of Jerusalem so that we will no longer be a reproach. (Nehemiah 2:17)

In my Bible, I've circled three vitally important words in verse 17: *we, us,* and *we.* For Nehemiah to motivate the city planning commission and potential employees, he had to identify himself with the need. Imagine the kind of response he would have received if he had said, "You folks have gotten yourselves into a bad mess. You know what you need to do? You need to rebuild that wall. If you need me, I'll be in my office. After all, I wasn't part of the problem. You people will have to get with it and do the work!"

When you cast blame and criticism, you squelch motivation. When you identify with the problem, you encourage motivation.

While Nehemiah identified with the people and was personally concerned about the problem, he did not hide the hard facts. He didn't plead or threaten, nor was he negative in his approach. He simply said, "We've got to do something about this problem. Let's rebuild the wall." Nehemiah extended the invitation to rebuild the wall and gave the people a persuasive reason for accepting it: ". . . so that we will no longer be a reproach."

There are two kinds of motivation: *extrinsic motivation,* which is the most common but used by fewer great leaders, and *intrinsic motivation.* Consider the use of extrinsic motivation. You say to your child, "Come on, Honey, it's time to get your bath. Let's clean up." And the child answers, "I don't want to." You respond, "I'll let you watch TV if you hurry."

There is a type of extrinsic motivation which must also employ some external incentive. When the child gets a little older and starts to school he may be told by his parents, "For every 'A' you make, we'll give you a dollar." When that same child enters college, he is told, "If you make good grades, you'll get on the dean's list." Again, that's extrinsic motivation. In the business community, there is the Christmas bonus or special trip to Hawaii that may be earned by increasing sales volume. That's scratching people where they itch—externally.

Intrinsic motivation, on the other hand, appeals to the inner person. Researchers point to several different internal factors that drive motivation, such as challenge, hope, competition, cooperation, and the desire for control or recognition. A person driven by intrinsic motivation would increase sales volume to enjoy the satisfaction of a job well done, to feel the thrill of accomplishment, or to experience a sense of community with fellow employees. Internal motivation tends to favor long-term, altruistic rewards, while extrinsic motivation tends to seek short-term, self-interested satisfaction.

This is not to suggest that all external or extrinsic motivation is wrong. Sometimes that's what people need. Children, especially, need to be rewarded for a job well done because it's all they may be capable of understanding. However, as we involve ourselves in developing their character, intrinsic motivation should have greater appeal. People under a great deal of stress also need more external motivation to help them get to a place where they can, again, appreciate the more altruistic, long-term intrinsic rewards.

I can spot a good leader when I see how he or she motivates others. First, wise leaders know the people in their charge and what will appeal to them. Second, wise leaders apply both extrinsic and intrinsic motivation in the right combination to keep others moving toward the right objective. Third, wise leaders favor intrinsic motivation, using external factors only as needed for the situation or to encourage intrinsic motivation.

Nehemiah didn't promise material incentives when he addressed the Jerusalem officials. He didn't offer prizes to the fastest-working families or a week at the Dead Sea for the group doing the most attractive work. Nehemiah simply said, "See the ruins? We're in a terrible strait. Let's rebuild this wall." And the people said, "Let's do it."

Why did the citizens respond in willingness to Nehemiah's proposal? Being led by God, Nehemiah was able to appeal to their *intrinsic* zeal. He was able to scratch them where they itched deep inside. There aren't many people who can do that today; there never have been. But they make the best leaders.

I have always been impressed with the life of Winston Churchill. In Churchill's speeches, I cannot find a time in which he ever employed extrinsic motivation. Listen to the words he spoke as England prepared to confront Nazi Germany just three days after Hitler rapidly occupied Belgium, France, and Holland:

I would say to the House, as I said to those who have joined this Government: "I have nothing to offer but blood, toil, tears and sweat."

We have before us an ordeal of the most grievous kind. We have before us many, many long months of struggle and of suffering. You ask, what is our policy? I can say: It is to wage war, by sea, land and air, with all our might and with all the strength that God can give us; to wage war against a monstrous tyranny, never surpassed in the dark, lamentable catalogue of human crime. That is our policy. You ask, what is our aim? I can answer in one word: It is victory, victory at all costs, victory in spite of all terror, victory, however long and hard the road may be; for without victory, there is no survival.[1]

Later, after the bombs fell and it appeared Great Britain would have to stand alone against Hitler, he declared:

We shall not flag or fail. We shall go on to the end, we shall fight in France, we shall fight on the seas and oceans, we shall fight with growing confidence and growing strength in the air, we shall defend our Island, whatever the cost may be, we shall fight on the beaches, we shall fight on the landing grounds, we shall fight in the fields and in the streets, we shall fight in the hills; we shall never surrender.[2]

And I will never forget the amazing speech he gave to a very fearful people in Britain when he addressed the House of Commons on December 30, 1941. It included these words:

When I warned [the French] that Britain would fight on alone whatever they did, their generals told their Prime Minister and his divided Cabinet, "In three weeks England will have her neck wrung like a chicken." Some chicken; some neck.[3]

The Nazis never wrung England's neck. Somehow Churchill, stubby little creature that he was, could stand in front of a microphone and strengthen Brits by the thousands with intrinsic motivation. He appealed to their inner strength, their sense of right and wrong, and to their zeal.

I'm reminded of David when he put off the armor of Saul and looked into the face of that ugly giant across the valley. He said, "Is there not a cause?" And while everybody else stood around figuring the odds, David thought, "Get out of the way!" He picked up a few rocks, and you know the rest of the story. David possessed that marvelous inner motivation never to surrender. It was that same inner strength and commitment that Nehemiah communicated:

I told them how the hand of my God had been favorable to me
. . . Then they said, "Let us arise and build." So they put their
hands to the good work. (Nehemiah 2:18)

Someone once suggested, "If you really want to check the leadership of an individual, just see if anybody's following." It was at this point that Nehemiah emerged as a leader. His new followers said, "Let's build. Let's put our hands to the good work."

With Motivation, Inevitable Opposition

Notice that right away opposition comes! It never fails. There is direct criticism of the plan. As soon as the rebuilding crews rolled up their sleeves, they were opposed. Murphy's Law could again be heard:

But when Sanballat the Horonite, and Tobiah the Ammonite official, and Geshem the Arab heard it, they mocked us and despised us. . . . (Nehemiah 2:19)

The Hebrew term for *mock* means "to stammer, to stutter, to utter repeatedly words of derision." Sanballat and Tobiah held their heads high, looked down their noses, and scoffed at that little group of Jews, saying, "You're out of your minds. You'll never be able to do it. After all, you're rebelling against the king, aren't you?"

I can see Nehemiah once again whip out those letters! "Here are the words of the king," he could exclaim with confidence. "I have the official sanction of Artaxerxes." (Again, his careful planning paid dividends.) Then, Nehemiah issued a get-tough policy at just the right time.

So I answered them and said to them, "The God of heaven will give us success; therefore we His servants will arise and build, but you have no portion, right or memorial in Jerusalem." (Nehemiah 2:20)

Nehemiah knew that he and the people of Jerusalem were doing God's work, and he was not going to listen to anyone actively opposed to what he knew was right. And furthermore, he did not intend to associate with those who would hinder what was obviously of God. He was determined to allow no one but God to stop the work.

I wonder how many of us would have said, "You know, people really don't want a new wall. We can't go on with this project because the opposition is too powerful. They haven't had a wall here in more than one hundred and fifty years, and they've gotten used to living like this. There's just no use changing. Let's pack up and pull out." Nehemiah, however, planted his feet firmly and held to his original position.

Part of the unwritten job requirements for every leader is the ability to handle criticism. That's part of the leadership package. If you never get criticized, chances are you aren't getting anything done. A wise leader will evaluate the opposition in light of the spirit and attitude in which criticism is given. He or she will also consider the voice to which the opposition listens. If your critics listen to God's voice, you had better listen to them. But if they are marching to a different drumbeat, use the Nehemiah technique: "Look, they're not even in the same camp. Let's go right on."

And you know something? Those stubborn men who opposed Nehemiah's mission still didn't leave. They dogged his steps through the entire project, until the last stone was set in place! When it was halfway finished, they taunted, "A little old fox could knock down that wall" (see Nehemiah 4:3). But remember, they were now outside the wall shouting over it.

This portion of Nehemiah's story takes up very little space in the pages of Scripture, but look at the ground it covers! He arrived in Jerusalem a solitary man with the task of overcoming years of apathy and entrenched enemy resistance, not to mention the already daunting engineering challenge of rebuilding the wall. Leadership, unlike mere management, is all about constructive change. How he got this project started is a model for leaders who want to move their organization toward more successful directions. His methods included astute observation, careful planning, appropriate timing, savvy motivation, effective communication, and unwavering dedication to a clear vision. Is it any wonder he succeeded?

Most importantly, Nehemiah never wandered far from his God, which prepared him to handle one of the greatest challenges to effective leadership: criticism. That is where we're going in the next chapter.

FIVE

Knocked Down, but Not Knocked Out

No leader is exempt from criticism, and his humility will nowhere be seen more clearly than in the manner in which he accepts and reacts to it.[1]

Anyone who steps into the arena of leadership must be prepared to pay a price. True leadership exacts a heavy toll on the whole person—and the more effective the leadership, the higher the price. The leader must soon face the fact that he will be the target of critical darts. Unpleasant though it may sound, you haven't really led until you have become familiar with the stinging barbs of the critic. That implies one thing: good leaders must have thick skin.

We left Nehemiah struggling with such criticism at the close of the previous chapter. It was intentional. Knowing that his critics were not through, I chose to deal with them at length in this chapter, rather than attempt a brief and hurried analysis earlier. But before we delve into the growing problem of opposition faced by Nehemiah, let's look at an unusual promise found in 2 Corinthians 4.

Anyone who is serious about serving God as a leader in the church of Jesus Christ should make a serious study of Paul the apostle. Paul's life offers a pattern that people in leadership should follow. Second Corinthians is a key book for study because he talks more about himself in this book than in any of his others.

We should not be surprised to read an honest admission about the toll of the ministry in Paul's life:

But we have this treasure in earthen vessels, so that the surpassing greatness of the power will be of God and not from ourselves. (2 Corinthians 4:7)

"We have this treasure in earthen vessels" refers to an earthenware jar, a clay pot. He was describing the treasure of the gospel, saying that it is housed in a clay jar, meaning our humanity. "We have this treasure [the gospel] in earthen vessels [our frail human bodies] that the surpassing greatness of the power will be of God and not from ourselves." There is no power or tenacity in a clay pot. It is fragile and plain. It often leaks. The passing of time only makes the vessel weaker. Paul was saying that any manifestation of power comes not from the pot, but rather from what the pot contains.

Next, Paul describes the life of frail human vessels:

We are afflicted in every way, but not crushed; perplexed, but not despairing; persecuted, but not forsaken; struck down, but not destroyed; always carrying about in the body the dying of

Jesus, so that the life of Jesus also may be manifested in our body.
(2 Corinthians 4:8–10)

Always is the key word in verse 10. Here, Paul described the life of the spiritual leader as "always carrying about in the body the dying of Jesus." The marks of death are always on the lives of people God uses.

These marks of death are evident in the lives of God's leaders because God wants to display the life of Jesus in the pot. You see, God is interested not only in blessing that which is in the pot, but also in using the pot itself. God doesn't declare abstract truth from the lips of an angel; He puts truth in real life. Then He brings that life before people, whether it is in business, a Bible class, a group of disciples, a growing Christian school, a mission organization, or a church. He uses imperfect people—clay pots—to display the glory of God. It is also emphasized in this passage that opposition is inevitable. A godly leader always carries the telltale marks of death.

I love the way J. B. Phillips puts the same verse together in his *Letters to Young Churches*. He writes:

We are handicapped on all sides but we are never frustrated: we are puzzled, but never in despair. We are persecuted, but we never have to stand it alone: we may be knocked down but we are never knocked out![2]

THE PRESENCE OF OPPOSITION

As we look again at Nehemiah, keep in mind that for the leader, opposition is inevitable. Nehemiah had one task, and that was to build a wall around the city of Jerusalem. It doesn't sound very spiritual, but it was God's will for his life.

In the process of that task, Nehemiah was led by God to appoint workmen for various parts of the project. Some were to build certain gates; some, a section of the wall. Some were to build in the south; others, up north of the city. But everybody had a job to do. The delegation of labor is described in elaborate detail in chapter 3 of the Book of Nehemiah.

Shortly thereafter, we read about the opposition that Nehemiah faced while the people of Jerusalem built the wall. God's will didn't allow the project to be completed without opposition. Before the wall was half finished, the sarcastic words of critics bombarded the workers:

> Now it came about that when Sanballat heard that we were rebuilding the wall, he became furious. (Nehemiah 4:1)

What prompted the opposition was the progress in the construction project. One would think that seeing this small band of people succeeding in a massive project would evoke admiration. But this was not so. You see, the heart of the habitual critic resists change. To him or her, change is a threat. In any organization, those who are most critical of change are those who are most inflexible. They resist change, and they become especially suspicious of changes that lead to progress and growth.

It was the change—the growth—that incited Sanballat's anger. Notice also the others involved in the opposition. After Sanballat heard about rebuilding the wall in verse 1, "He spoke in the presence of his brothers and the wealthy men of Samaria . . . Now Tobiah the Ammonite was near him . . ." (Nehemiah 4:2–3). I point this out to emphasize something that is usually true: Critics run with critics. And obviously while not all criticism is of the devil, this criticism was. It was destructive and disturbing.

Every leader must develop the ability to measure the value or worth of criticism. He has to determine the source and the motive, and he has to listen with discernment. Sometimes the best course of action is to graciously accept the criticism and learn from it. Other times, it must be strongly resisted.

Nehemiah's critics were constantly in agreement with one another, and their reaction was not a quiet, mildly disinterested one. No, they were angry! They became sarcastic. Look at the sarcasm in verse 3. "Now Tobiah the Ammonite was near him [Sanballat] and he said, 'Even what they are building—if a fox should jump on it, he would break their stone wall down!' "

Can you imagine a comment like that? But Tobiah made a crucial mistake. He claimed that a mere fox "would break their stone wall down." But what they built was not "their" stone wall. The Lord wanted the wall built. He happened to use Nehemiah as the construction superintendent, but God commissioned the work and owned the final product. Carping critics typically look at situations from a human point of view—*their* walls, *their* plans, *their* comfort, *their* procedure, *their* arrangement—usually wrapping their derision in carefully crafted logic or, even worse, cleverly contorted Scripture. They don't stop to think that they may be criticizing God's project.

People who look at life from the human point of view have problems with projects that require giant steps of faith. We as leaders who are Christian need to ask ourselves, "Am I really looking to God for vision, for growth, and for direction, or am I taking the easy way out, allowing the status quo to earn approval from my peers and to keep my position secure?" If we earnestly and genuinely seek God's best for our lives, we must learn to keep our eyes open and our attitudes positive—not lacking in discernment, but remaining focused and positive. And we must never forget that those who are, by nature, negative and critical will always, *always* be around to create opposition. Nevertheless, the work must go on. Progress should not stop because a loud minority wants to disparage us or hinder the plan.

FACING CRITICISM SQUARELY

Let's call this what it is: spiritual warfare. And battles of that sort are best fought from a kneeling position. When those sidewalk supervisors tried to disrupt construction of the Jerusalem wall, Nehemiah responded to the criticism in two significant ways: He prayed and he persisted.

First, *he talked to God about the criticism.* Take note of his unusual prayer.

> Hear, O our God, how we are despised! Return their reproach on their own heads and give them up for plunder in a land of captivity. Do not forgive their iniquity and let not their sin be blotted out before You, for they have demoralized the builders. (Nehemiah 4:4–5)

This is rare! The Bible is filled with "forgive our iniquities," "forgive us our sins," "relieve us of our transgressions," and "cover our transgressions"—but Nehemiah prayed, "*Don't* forgive their iniquity" and "*Let not* their sin be blotted out before You, for they have demoralized the builders." While this may not be a model prayer theologically, I highly commend its honesty!

Please keep in mind that Nehemiah was a great man and a leader we would do well to emulate. He was outraged at the conduct of the critics and he said some very rash things . . . in the privacy and security of his prayer closet. As we have seen before, Nehemiah was a man of prayer. He spent untold hours on his knees, giving vent to his frustrations and his anger, saying to the Lord—in the safety of prayer—what he wanted to say to his critics and to others. Prayer is a great way to unpack our frustrations.

Leaders are often people who have very strong wills. They need this internal drive to overcome the inertia of doubt, fear of change, and criticism. Unfortunately, this quality can make retaliation the most natural response to attack. Building a wall around Jerusalem required someone with Nehemiah's get-tough mind-set. And with opponents like these, it would have been quite understandable if Nehemiah had punched out a few lights. But he didn't go that far.

For the sake of emphasis, let me repeat a very important principle. You are never more successful than when you make your plans, advance your cause, and overcome your obstacles on your knees in prayer. The leader who advances on his knees need never retreat. When responding to critics, begin with prayer, then give a response only as the situation compels it.

Proverbs 15:1 says, "A gentle answer turns away wrath, but a harsh word stirs up anger." What do we do when a harsh word is spoken to us? We usually shout louder. Think about your most recent argument. It went on as long as it did because both of you kept adding a comment after the other's. If you want to stop an argument, simply apply Proverbs 15:1 and close your mouth. The other person will usually just run out of gas. If you want to keep the argument going, answer the complaint or criticism in a harsh way. Look at verses 28 and 29 in the same chapter of Proverbs:

> The heart of the righteous ponders how to answer,
> But the mouth of the wicked pours out evil things.
> The Lord is far from the wicked,
> But He hears the prayer of the righteous.
> (Proverbs 15:28–29)

Before Nehemiah said a word to his critics, he talked with His God. He refused to retaliate even though others might have encouraged him to do so. Good for him!

When I was serving the Lord in a church in Waltham, Massachusetts, there was a church in the same area that had an amazing history. One pastor inherited a terrible mess when he first arrived to lead the congregation. Attendance was down, and those who did attend sat in the back three pews. On this pastor's first Sunday, he picked up the pulpit and dragged it down the aisle, placing it near the people. He responded to criticism much the same way, with humor and creativity. With each passing Sunday, the pews filled, forcing him to move the pulpit more and more toward the front of the sanctuary. Before long, he was almost perched in the choir loft! He preached the Word, walked with God, and faithfully labored in spite of opposition. Eventually, God chose to call him to a school that has consistently moved ahead under his guidance.

His successor was a retaliatory man, a fighter. This man held more than one graduate degree; he was absolutely brilliant. He was a well-traveled, well-read, experienced leader of people, seemingly with a lot more going for him than the other fellow. Like his predecessor, this pastor received criticism and hostility from certain segments of the church membership, and week by week, one public argument and retaliatory action after another, the church systematically emptied. Sure, he won the arguments, but he lost the people.

One man fought on his knees, the other on his feet.

Retrain your reflexes. Let your first response to criticism be an honest, cathartic, soul-cleansing season of prayer—take as long as you need. (Let's face it; some of your critics may require your spending weeks on your knees!) Speak as little in response as you possibly can. Ask the Lord to deal with your critics His way and in His time. Remain focused on your objective. In time, you will find, as I have, that you are never used by God more effectively than when you are praying for your critics.

THE NEED FOR COMMON SENSE

Nehemiah's second response to criticism: *He stayed on task.* He persisted. I love what Nehemiah wrote in chapter 4, verse 6: "So we built the wall." The words of criticism fell like rain, yet he continued on. I can just hear him. "Keep mixing the mortar and hand me another brick!"

> So we built the wall and the whole wall was joined together to half
> its height, for the people had a mind to work. (Nehemiah 4:6)

Critics demoralize. Leaders encourage. When the critics spoke, the workmen heard them and were demoralized. But when their leader stepped up and said, "Let's look at it God's way; stay with the job," the crew members were back in there with those trowels and wheelbarrows, putting together the stone and the mortar, building the gates and the hinges.

Nothing excites the adversary or the critic more than for his negativism to hinder the progress of something good. And nothing frustrates him more than when we find renewed strength in the Lord to persist. But let's not kid ourselves. Satan won't give up and go away.

Nehemiah said, "Stay at the task. Don't give up. Keep building." You could hear the workmen day and night, slapping on mortar and setting stones. That productive activity should have assaulted the hearts of Sanballat, Tobiah, and Geshem—but that's not the case. In fact, the size of their group grew. Verses 7 and 8 tell us that Sanballat and Tobiah were joined by the Ammonites and the Ashodites, and they even added some Arabs! They intensified the opposition. And when they

> heard that the repair of the walls of Jerusalem went on, and that
> the breaches began to be closed, they were very angry. All of
> them conspired together to come and fight against Jerusalem
> and to cause a disturbance in it. (Nehemiah 4:7–8)

Sometimes criticism doesn't die down—it intensifies. Not only did the critics expand their troops, but they added intensity to the opposition. They planned a conspiracy and arranged to cause a disturbance. What did Nehemiah do when confronted with continued harassment? As was his custom, he intensified his prayer: "But we prayed to our God, and because of them we set up a guard against them day and night" (Nehemiah 4:9). The intensified opposition might have knocked him down, but it was a long way from knocking him out.

Intensified opposition against the will of God calls for an intensified response. Nehemiah not only heard the opposition, but he also analyzed available data, prayed, and took decisive, practical action. He set up a guard against them, which was a common-sense response. He persisted by taking up arms.

Occasionally persistence in the form of common sense must prevail. Do you fear that someone is going to break into your home? Certainly you should trust God, but don't forget to lock the doors. Don't just pray about it. It is foolish to leave doors unlocked when you are praying that your home will not be burglarized.

Out of a job? Pray! But pound the pavement too. Send out the resume. Make contacts. Get in touch with as many opportunities as possible. The Lord doesn't have any trouble guiding a moving target. In fact, it's easier to steer a moving vehicle than one that is immobile.

We will read more about Nehemiah's common sense in the next chapter, but I don't want us to miss three very practical truths that can be gleaned from Nehemiah 4.

1. *It is impossible to lead anyone without facing opposition.* The leader must learn to take the heat. He will face opposition—it's an occupational hazard of every leadership position. Darts will come your way.

2. *It is essential to face opposition in prayer.* The first response to opposition must be prayer. Prayer is the single, most often overlooked discipline in the Christian life among leaders.

3. *Prayer is not all that is necessary if opposition grows.* That was true of David. He prayed when Saul was after him, but he also ran like mad! When opposition intensified, he ran faster. When it got worse, he hid in more obscure places. In many cases, the critic isn't worth the worry. But if the leader has prayed and is still facing intensified opposition, he or she must use common sense.

Many years ago, I became discouraged because of criticism and my optimism eroded as a lengthy chain of events led me into "the pits." Knowing of my need for encouragement, my wife searched for a way to lift my spirits. She found these encouraging comments written by a statesman I have always admired, and used them on a wooden decoupage plaque she gave to me. Consider the words of Theodore Roosevelt:

It is not the critic who counts; not the man who points out how the strong man stumbles, or where the doer of deeds could have done them better. The credit belongs to the man who is actually in the arena, whose face is marred by dust and sweat and blood; who strives valiantly; who errs, and comes short again and again, because there is no effort without error and shortcoming; but who does actually strive to do the deeds; who knows the great enthusiasms, the great devotions; who spends himself in a worthy cause; who at the best knows in the end the triumph of high achievement, and who at the worst, if he fails, at least fails while daring greatly.[3]

Far better it is to dare mighty things, to win glorious triumphs, even though checkered by failure, than to take rank with those poor spirits who neither enjoy much nor suffer much, because they live in the gray twilight that knows not victory nor defeat.[4]

I repeat the opening statement of this chapter: no leader is exempt from criticism. Don't expect to be. But when it comes, be ready to battle against discouragement, which is poised and ready to strike on the heels of criticism. You can count on it!

Six

Discouragement: Its Causes and Cure

Edith, a mother of eight in Darlington, Maryland, was coming home from a neighbor's house one Saturday afternoon. As she walked into the house, she saw five of her youngest children huddled together, concentrating with intense interest on something. As she slipped near them, trying to discover the center of attention, she couldn't believe her eyes. Smack-dab in the middle of the circle was a group of baby skunks. She screamed at the top of her voice, "Children, run!" *Then each kid grabbed a skunk and ran!*[1]

When I first read that true story in John Haggai's *How to Win Over Worry*, I thought of Nehemiah. Like that mother, he had no idea how complicated life could get. He took on a project that had all the appearance of being harmless, innocent, and rather simple. After all, what could be so difficult about building a wall around a city? It seemed that Nehemiah could have that wall completed in just a few weeks; then he would go back to Persia and take up where he left off. But not so!

He looked over the shoulders of those workmen, and it was like suddenly confronting a living room full of skunks! In fact, the more he tried to alleviate the problem, the greater it became. First he faced sarcasm, then mockery, which led to open opposition, criticism, and finally conspiracy. In fact, the conspiracy became so great that before long the inevitable took place—discouragement threatened to kill the project. No matter how hard he tried, Nehemiah was unable to correct the problems. They only grew worse, multiplying and magnifying with each passing day. Finally, as he shouted, "Keep building!" each workman grabbed a skunk and ran!

I suppose all of us, in some measure, have experienced a situation like Edith's or Nehemiah's. While trying to solve a problem, it grew worse right before our eyes. The problem that plagued Nehemiah was that of discouragement. I know of few afflictions more persistent than discouragement. It's like a debilitating disease. Rare is the person who can resist or overcome it alone.

Thomas Edison's son, Charles, penned a brief, yet stimulating biography of his father, one that reveals the great inventor's contagious determination and optimism.

I especially recall a freezing December night in 1914, at a time when still unfruitful experiments on the nickel-iron-alkaline storage battery, to which Father had devoted much of ten years, had put him on a financial tightrope. Only profits from movie and record production were supporting the laboratory. On that December evening the cry of "Fire!" echoed through the plant. Spontaneous combustion had broken out in the film room. Within moments all the packing compounds, celluloid for records, film and other flammable goods had gone up with a whoosh. Fire companies from eight towns arrived, but the heat was so intense, and the water pressure so low, that the fire hoses had no effect.

When I couldn't find Father, I became concerned. Was he safe? With all his assets going up in smoke, would his spirit be broken? He was 67, no age to begin anew. Then I saw him in the plant yard, running toward me.

"Where's Mom?" he shouted, "Go get her! Tell her to get her friends! They'll never see a fire like this again!"

At 5:30 the next morning, with the fire barely under control, he called his employees together and announced, "We're rebuilding." One man was told to lease all the machine shops in the area. Another, to obtain a wrecking crane from the Erie Railroad Company. Then, almost as an afterthought he added, "Oh, by the way. Anybody know where we can get some money?"

Later on he explained, "You can always make capital out of disaster. We've just cleared out a bunch of old rubbish. We'll build bigger and better on the ruins." With that he rolled up his coat for a pillow, curled up on a table and immediately fell asleep.[2]

Thanks to the "Wizard of Menlo Park," we enjoy the microphone, the stereo, the incandescent light, the storage battery, talking movies, and more than a thousand other inventions. In addition to being a technological genius, he refused to be discouraged.

Nehemiah, like Edison, faced insurmountable odds, but he refused to be overtaken and paralyzed by discouragement.

SOURCE OF DISCOURAGEMENT

Before we consider either the causes or the cures for this affliction, notice the source of Nehemiah's problem—the people of Judah (see Nehemiah 4:10). Way back in the last chapters of Genesis, we discover that Judah was not just any tribe among the people of Israel. Judah was the leader.

In Genesis 49, we read that Jacob summoned his sons before him and set before them a series of blessings, warnings, predictions, and discouragements. When he came to Judah (see Genesis 49:8), he predicted that Judah's descendents would become the tribe of kings. Then he added, "The scepter shall not depart from Judah, nor the ruler's staff from between his feet, until Shiloh comes" (Genesis 49:10). (Shiloh means literally, "the peaceful one," indicating the future Messiah.)

Jacob said, in effect, "Judah, yours will be the Messianic tribe. Through your tribe, the Savior of the world, the Messiah, will be born. The scepter will never depart from you. And to Him [to Shiloh] shall be the obedience of all people." These people of Judah were to be respected because they were the chosen ones through whom the Lord Jesus would someday be born.

But when you get to Nehemiah 4, you find that the discouraging words come from the tribe of Judah, of all people. Eugene Peterson's paraphrase of the Bible, *The Message*, expresses the urgency of the discouragement well.

And all this time our enemies were saying, "They won't know what hit them. Before they know it we'll be at their throats, killing them right and left. That will put a stop to the work!"

The Jews who were their neighbors kept reporting, "They have us surrounded; they're going to attack!" If we heard it once, we heard it ten times. (Nehemiah 4:11–12 MSG)

Let me point out that the discouraging information was channeled through people who lived in close proximity to its source. *You cannot constantly hear negativism without having some of it rub off on you.* If you are prone to discouragement, you shouldn't run the risk of spending a lot of your time with people who traffic in discouraging information. Nehemiah's discouragement came first from Judah, which was very surprising, and next from those Jews who lived near the critics—which was very significant.

CAUSES OF DISCOURAGEMENT

If we look closely, we will discover four causes for Nehemiah's discouragement.

1. *A loss of strength.* Verse 10 reads, "Thus in Judah it was said, 'The strength of the burden bearers is failing.'" The word rendered "failing" reads "stumbling, tottering, staggering" in the original text. In other words, "These people, Nehemiah, have been working a long time, and they are getting tired." Verse 6 tells us they were halfway through the project, which means that the excitement of starting a new venture had worn off. In fact, many experienced project managers have identified this tendency as a normal stage in the typical project life cycle:

- Enthusiasm

- Disillusionment

- Panic

- Search for the Guilty

- Punishment of the Innocent

- Praise for the Nonparticipants

The midpoint of a long, demanding project is prime time for discouragement. The disillusionment phase occurs after the momentum of a great start peters out and long before the anticipation of the finish line can inspire hope. It's the time when the resilient must put their heads down and keep their feet moving and when the weary need an infusion of encouragement.

2. *A loss of vision.* Did you notice what Judah said? "Yet there is much rubbish" (Nehemiah 4:10). The word "yet" is significant because it connects the thought with the previous statement. The burden bearers' strength had begun to fail; yet, in spite of all the work, there's a lot of rubble. The Hebrew-translated rubbish means "dry earth, debris." Lying all around the workers are piles of debris— dirt, broken stones, dried chunks of mortar.

Rubbish and discouragement perfectly complement one another to flatten morale.

My wife, Cynthia, and I just completed a move into our new house close to Stonebriar Community Church where I am the senior pastor. Even as I edit the manuscript for this book, I am surrounded by countless cartons and cardboard boxes. Half the shelves in my library are empty; many of my books are still packed. Only recently have we cleared away enough room to sit in the living room, and the kitchen is a clattering chaos of pots, pans, spice bottles, small appliances, and . . . I'm exhausted just describing it! And while we could barely contain our excitement upon receiving the keys to our new home, I must confess that the disorder sometimes sunk my mood. The confusion of all that clutter often obscured the beauty of the house we are blessed to call home.

Slowly but surely, though, the boxes are being emptied and carried out to the recycle bin. I freely confess that my optimism grows with the restoration of order.

3. *A loss of confidence.* When people lose confidence in their ability to accomplish a task, or in the merit of the objective, or in the approval and presence of God, discouragement is the inevitable result. The top of the wall stood barely taller than the piles of rubble that lined the site, which gave the appearance that little progress had been made. The wearied people began to whine, "We ourselves are unable to rebuild the wall" (Nehemiah 4:10).

These Jews had built the wall to half its height because the people "had a mind to work" (Nehemiah 4:6). The Hebrew reads, ". . . the people had a heart to work." But now *they have lost heart.* The loss of strength and vision leads to the loss of confidence. And with the loss of confidence, discouragement is not far behind.

4. *A loss of security.* The final cause for discouragement in the case of these Jews was a growing insecurity. Verse 11 reads, "Our enemies said, 'They will not know or see until we come among them, kill them, and put a stop to the work.'" When the workers heard of the plot and realized how serious their enemies were, they suddenly slumped into discouragement. They lost their sense of safety.

Security is undoubtedly a basic human need that cannot be ignored or minimized. People typically find it difficult to concentrate on anything, regardless how meaningful it might be, when they fear for their safety. However, we must not mistake the true source of security. Our natural tendency is to seek tangible sources rather than the faith-oriented rest the Lord wants us to find in Him. For instance, if someone needs a steady income to feel secure, then all he needs is to lose that job for discouragement to swamp him.

Another familiar security blanket is close friends and familiar circumstances. A move to some other part of the country threatens that. Let's say, for example, that your spouse comes home tomorrow afternoon and says, "Honey, the company wants to move us to Bangor, Maine."

"Bangor, Maine? What in the world is in Bangor, Maine?"

Everything you know and love surrounds your current location. You've never been beyond your secure backyard. Your whole lifestyle is determined by your longtime residence where you now live. Your "roots" are being loosened. All the tangibles that you've hung on to for security are threatened. After a few weeks in unfamiliar territory, away from all the things that gave you the illusion of safety, discouragement can set in.

You might think that discouragement is only for those not walking with God. That's not true. Many Christian leaders admit that times of discouragement have often been signals from God announcing a whole new direction and plan. Strange though it may seem, discouragement, brought on by a removal of our tangible securities, can become the catalyst for incredible achievements.

Such was the admission of Charles Haddon Spurgeon, one of the greatest spokesmen for Christ in the history of the church.

> Before any great achievement, some measure of the same depression is very usual. . . . Such was my experience when I first became a pastor in London. My success appalled me; and the thought of the career which it seemed to open up, so far from elating me, cast me into the lowest depth, out of which I uttered my *miserere* and found no room for a *gloria in excelsis*. Who was I that I should continue to lead so great a multitude? I would betake me to my village obscurity, or emigrate to America, and find a solitary nest in the backwoods, where I might be sufficient for the things that would be demanded of me. It was just then the curtain was rising on my lifework. . . . This depression comes over me whenever the Lord is preparing a larger blessing for my ministry.[3]

I can find nothing in Scripture to prove this, but I am more convinced than ever that discouragement is nothing more than a barrier Satan erects between great people and great achievements. I wonder how many great triumphs we might have seen but didn't because great people simply lost heart.

Perhaps today you find yourself standing before the door of opportunity or change. Your strength has run out. Your confidence has faded. Your vision has grown dim. You're shaking with fear and you want to retreat to safety. A nagging voice somewhere deep within whispers, "It isn't worth it."

Wait! You may be on the verge of the greatest years of your life.

On the other side of that barrier—if you just keep pressing on, doing what you know to be right—the reward of faithfulness awaits you.

How Can We Deal with Discouragement?

Building that Jerusalem wall turned out to be more difficult than anyone imagined! Discouragement ran rampant. Satan must have been having a field day. Nevertheless, Nehemiah didn't allow discouragement to go unanswered. (You can't ignore discouragement any more than you can ignore a flat tire. Pray all you want to; drive all you want to; but a flat tire won't fix itself. So it is with discouragement.) He rolled up his sleeves like a good leader and dealt with it head-on. I find five strategies he employed that worked for him and still work today.

1. *Unify your efforts toward a goal.* The first thing Nehemiah did was rally the people around the goal.

> Then I stationed men in the lowest parts of the space behind the wall, the exposed places, and I stationed the people in families with their swords, spears, and bows. (Nehemiah 4:13)

How significant! The builders had been scattered all over Jerusalem, working together with stones, water, and mortar, *yet separated from their families.* Nehemiah unified them according to families and gave each one a common goal—preservation. He turned their attention from themselves to the enemy, from the discouragement of self-pity to the goal of self-preservation. He "tightened the ranks" and thereby encouraged the disheartened.

Notice what happened in the process of uniting the people:

Nehemiah *stopped the work.* Sometimes the very best thing to do when people are discouraged is to take some time off. An old Greek proverb says, "You will break the bow if you keep it always bent." How tight is your bow? When is the last time you loosened the string and halted the work for a couple of days?

Workaholics make poor workers and worse leaders. Nehemiah stopped the work and said, "Let's pull together." That will provide encouragement to disheartened people.

2. *Direct your attention to the Lord.* Next, Nehemiah directed the attention of the people to the Lord and away from the rubble.

> When I saw their fear, I rose and spoke to the nobles, the officials and the rest of the people: "Do not be afraid of them; remember the Lord who is great and awesome, and fight for your brothers, your sons, your daughters, your wives and your houses." (Nehemiah 4:14)

I love how Nehemiah stood up and took charge. That's leadership on parade! He directed the attention of the people away from the enemies and the obstacles and had them refocus on their God and the reasons for their labor.

How do we "remember the Lord?" By *calling to mind the things the Lord has said.* By reading and meditating on His Word. Even better if you commit portions of it to memory so you can call them up and apply them on the spot. Consider the following two examples:

> The steadfast of mind You will keep in perfect peace,
> Because he trusts in You.

Trust in the Lord forever,

For in God the Lord, we have an everlasting Rock.

(Isaiah 26:3–4)

Be anxious for nothing, but in everything by prayer and suppli-
cation with thanksgiving let your requests be made known to
God. And the peace of God, which surpasses all comprehension,
will guard your hearts and your minds in Christ Jesus.
(Philippians 4:6–7)

You remember the Lord by remembering what the Lord has said.
Commit to memory five or six solid promises like these that you can
recall and apply when afflicted by discouragement. When the devil
attacks, are you ready to mount a counterattack with living words?
Are you able to wield the sword of the Spirit, God's Word?

We can also "remember the Lord" by *calling to mind who He is.*
When is the last time you reflected upon the greatness of God? Perhaps
it was while lying flat on your back, looking up at the stars. Do you
ever get in your car and drive to a secluded spot just to find some quiet
time alone with God? That often helps clear away the fog and enables
the mind to recall God's incalculable strength, His boundless love, and
His steadfast faithfulness. Equally essential are those occasions when
Christians come together at the Lord's Table. Communion is God's
"show and tell" time, revealing anew the wonder of His Person.

3. *Maintain a balance between faith and action.* Once Nehemiah
refocused the people's attention on the Lord and the task, once he
reoriented their thinking, he urged them to resume building the
wall. However, his urging didn't ignore the very real danger of attack.

While he encouraged them to look to the Lord for their security, he also ordered them to maintain a proper defense as they accomplished the work by faith. Note Nehemiah's response to the safety issue:

> When I saw their fear, I rose and spoke to the nobles, the officials and the rest of the people: "Do not be afraid of them; remember the Lord who is great and awesome [Faith], and fight for your brothers, your sons, your daughters, your wives and your houses [Action]." When our enemies heard that it was known to us, and that God had frustrated their plan, then all of us returned to the wall, each one to his work [Faith]. From that day on, half of my servants carried on the work while half of them held the spears, the shields, the bows and the breastplates; and the captains were behind the whole house of Judah [Action]. Those who were rebuilding the wall and those who carried burdens took their load with one hand doing the work [Faith] and the other holding a weapon [Action]. (Nehemiah 4:14–17)

That, my friend, is a timely illustration for the Christian life. We are called to action that is fueled by faith. Any worthwhile endeavor will involve both. Guard against the subtle teaching that suggests that God does everything and you step back and do nothing, or that using good, common sense is necessarily demonstrating a lack of faith. The Bible continually exhorts us to put our trust in the Lord to work in accomplishing His will.

4. *Determine a rallying point.* The fourth strategy that Nehemiah applied was to establish a rallying point. Observe what Nehemiah did.

I said to the nobles, the officials and the rest of the people, "The work is great and extensive, and we are separated on the wall far from one another. At whatever place you hear the sound of the trumpet, rally to us there. Our God will fight for us." (Nehemiah 4:19–20)

A rally point is a *place*, but it also suggests a *principle*. The trumpet would establish the place. Nehemiah ordered, "Whenever you hear that trumpet sound, run to the spot where the bugler stands." The purpose of the rally point is to ensure that the people face their attackers together. The principle: don't try to fight alone. To overcome discouragement, always face adversity together.

When Jezebel sought to kill Elijah, he became more disheartened than ever and fled into the desert.

He came to a lone broom bush and collapsed in its shade, wanting in the worst way to be done with it all—to just die: "Enough of this, God! Take my life—I'm ready to join my ancestors in the grave! . . . I've been working my heart out for the God-of-the-Angel-Armies," said Elijah. "The people of Israel have abandoned your covenant, destroyed the places of worship, and murdered your prophets. I'm the only one left, and now they're trying to kill me." (1 Kings 19:4, 10 MSG).

In response to Elijah's discouragement, the Lord nourished his body with food, then refreshed his spirit with the news that seven thousand other faithful Hebrews lived in Israel and that Elisha would become his protégé and companion in ministry. After this incident, Elijah's ministry really took off. He had found his rally point. God gave him a companion with whom he could be accountable (which is extremely important), bare his soul, share his hurts, and relieve his loneliness.

Leaders and followers alike need others upon whom they can rely as they face the inevitable difficulties of life. If you are a leader, establish a rally point where the people in your charge can connect and draw strength from one another. And by no means neglect this need in yourself. Find peers with whom you can share your sorrows, questions, frustrations, and insights.

5. *Develop a "serve-one-another" mentality.* Nehemiah's fifth and final strategy to combat discouragement among his people was to encourage them to serve one another.

> So we carried on the work with half of them holding spears from dawn until the stars appeared. At that time I also said to the people, "Let each man with his servant spend the night within Jerusalem so that they may be a guard for us by night and a laborer by day." (Nehemiah 4:21–22)

Nehemiah called for the people to take round-the-clock shifts in pairs to keep the whole company safe. Volunteers would have to sleep within the barely constructed walls to keep vandals from tearing down what they had built. Take note of how he jump-started the volunteering.

> So neither I, my brothers, my servants, nor the men of the guard who followed me, none of us removed our clothes, each took his weapon even to the water. (Nehemiah 4:23)

Now, that's a leader! He called for everyone to serve the others in both guard duty and construction. And I love how he, himself, took the lead. First to sign up for the longest hours and the toughest duty: Nehemiah, the chief servant.

How involved are you in the lives of others? If you are a leader, how much do you really care for the people in your organization—I mean as individuals? This week, how much of your life will be spent meeting the needs of another? Or is it all wrapped up in yourself? If we want to foster a spirit of service within the groups we lead, we must be the first to step out and model the behavior we hope to see. Each one of us should take a long look at our short lives, taking special note of our personal investment in the lives of others, especially the people we lead.

Discouragement is indeed a debilitating disease, but it need not become terminal. Left to itself, it can be. But remedies are available. As we've discovered, Nehemiah utilized at least five strategies to keep the people of Jerusalem on-task and on-target, helping them achieve more than they imagined and all they dared to hope for. Glance back over Nehemiah's experience and compare his set of circumstances to yours. Be honest as you carry out this next mental project. Do you detect the symptoms of discouragement in your organization? Think objectively. Review Nehemiah's five strategies and see how you might adapt them to your situation.

Don't allow the disease of discouragement to run its course. Otherwise, you'll never know what great things could have been accomplished.

SEVEN

Love, Loans . . . and the Money Crunch

Making sense with dollars is a basic task of any leader. Very few projects are accomplished without an outlay of cash. And when cash starts to flow, wisdom, honesty, self-control, accountability, and intelligent, realistic planning must prevail. Even Jesus addressed the importance of financial planning.

> Is there anyone here who, planning to build a new house, doesn't first sit down and figure the cost so you'll know if you can complete it? If you only get the foundation laid and then run out of money, you're going to look pretty foolish. Everyone passing by will poke fun at you: "He started something he couldn't finish." (Luke 14:28–30 MSG)

To our Lord, careful money management is not considered an optional luxury. It is an essential ingredient in the lives of those in leadership. Because the Book of Nehemiah illustrates nearly every major principle of leadership, we shouldn't be surprised to find that Nehemiah faced the money issue. We read of this in the fifth chapter of his book, and it seems so typical of our lives that we could think he is living in the twenty-first century.

A strike occurred among the laborers who had been building the Jerusalem wall. They probably didn't picket the site by carrying hand-painted signs and blocking traffic, but they stopped working and started grumbling about their conditions:

> Now there was a great outcry of the people and of their wives against their Jewish brothers. (Nehemiah 5:1)

"We've gone on strike!" they might have said. "It isn't fair. We have our rights!" They temporarily halted construction to voice their grievances. Nehemiah, like a good leader, sized up the situation as he listened to their gripes:

- Some had large families without enough to eat (see Nehemiah 5:2).

- Others owned property, yet had to mortgage their homes and property because of the spiraling inflation problem (see Nehemiah 5:3).

- Still others were heavily in debt, unable to pay back what they owed (see Nehemiah 5:4–5).

It was a miserable, panic-stricken situation. How could this have happened?

REASONS FOR THE CRUNCH

If we look carefully, we discover three reasons for the complaints in these same five verses.

1. *Famine.* Verse 3 reads, "We are mortgaging our fields, our vineyards, and our houses that we might get grain because of the famine." Why was there a problem? The city had not been tilled and cultivated to meet the demands of the hundreds of people who suddenly flooded into it to build the wall. The existing limited crop could not sustain them. In addition to the increased demand for food, the whole area was experiencing a famine, apparently caused by a drought.

2. *Taxes.* Artaxerxes was demanding a heavy tribute in excess of what the land could produce. Verse 4 reads, "We have borrowed money for the king's tax on our fields and our vineyards." Artaxerxes controlled most of the known world at that time, and the armies required to help him retain that control didn't fight for free. He taxed everyone living under his dominion, including these laborers living eight hundred miles from Persia. Furthermore, tax collectors in that day were notoriously corrupt, inflating the tax bill and pocketing the difference.

3. *Usury.* Those with enough cash to finance their neighbors' debts were demanding inappropriately high interest rates. In ancient times, the custom was to indenture oneself as a servant until the debt was paid. In other words, a man would exchange labor for enough cash to pay off his debt. He and, usually, his family with him would become the slaves of another for a period of time—but the creditors would charge so much interest that the borrower could never end his term of service.

> Now our flesh is like the flesh of our brothers, our children like their children. Yet behold, we are forcing our sons and our daughters to be slaves, and some of our daughters are forced into bondage already, and we are helpless because our fields and vineyards belong to others. (Nehemiah 5:5)

Before long, so many people had lost their freedom to never-ending servanthood that no one was left to work on the wall and the project ground to a halt. Eventually, the leader had to step in to get control of the city's failing economy. Nehemiah said, "Then I was very angry when I had heard their outcry and these words" (Nehemiah 5:6). When he saw they had stopped the job they were called to do, he was infuriated—especially when he discovered the real source of the problem.

When All Else Fails, Read the Instructions

Nehemiah was angry because the people had forgotten the Mosaic Law. Because we live in the era of grace, we tend to look disparagingly (unfortunately) on the Law. But we must remember that the Law the Lord gave Israel through Moses was an act of grace. It established the context of their relationship with Him. It taught them about their sinfulness and provided a way to approach Him for forgiveness. It provided them with a strong sense of unity and identity while living in a foreign land. And it preserved the people of Israel by telling them how to live with one another. God's band of twelve tribes was to live distinctly different than their neighbors as a result of His personalized instructions. His law gave the Jews standards for living a just and godly life as a family. However, the chosen nation barely held together in Nehemiah's day because the people failed to follow instructions. Ironically, the very nobles who wanted the wall built were undermining the process by enslaving their brothers.

Twenty-first-century Christians would also do well to pay close attention to God's guidelines. Notice these instructions in Exodus:

> If you lend money to My people, to the poor among you, you are not to act as a creditor to him; you shall not charge him interest. (Exodus 22:25)

Now, look at Deuteronomy 23:19–20:

> You shall not charge interest to your countrymen: interest on money, food, or anything that may be loaned at interest. You may charge interest to a foreigner, but to your countrymen you shall not charge interest, so that the Lord your God may bless you in all that you undertake in the land which you are about to enter to possess. (Deuteronomy 23:19–20)

Don't miss the promise God attaches to the command, which turns the issue into a matter of faith. In effect, He promised, "*If you obey*, I will bless you so much more than the interest you would gain by exploiting your own brothers." He wanted His people to maintain such a distinction as would cause a foreigner to stroke his beard and wonder, "Why is that nation so prosperous?" This, of course, would warrant the response, "The Lord, our God, provides our needs without the need to charge each other any interest."

In between Exodus and Deuteronomy is a passage in Leviticus 25 that may also have been in Nehemiah's mind.

> Now in case a countryman of yours [a fellow Jew] becomes poor and his means with regard to you falter, then you are to sustain him, like a stranger or a sojourner, that he may live with you. Do not take usurious interest from him, but revere your God, that your countryman may live with you. You shall not give him your silver at interest, nor your food for gain. [Don't give him one bushel of grain, expecting one and a half back; give him one for one.] I am the Lord your God, who brought you out of the land of Egypt to give you the land of Canaan and to be your God. If a countryman of yours becomes so poor with regard to you that he sells himself to you, you shall not subject him to a slave's service. He shall be with you as a hired man, as if he were a sojourner; he shall serve with you until the year of jubilee. (Leviticus 25:35–40)

No Jew was ever to enslave another Jew. Such action was evidence of an absence of love and concern for his brother. Their family love was to supersede love of money. God's instructions (which they willfully disobeyed) would have protected and preserved the Jews of Nehemiah's day during this period of stress. But because they chose their own problem-solving method, they sank into the quicksand of increasing compromise.

We know by Nehemiah's reaction to the people's complaints that he knew these four principles found in the Law:

• It is *not* wrong to lend money to a non-Jew for interest.

- It is *not* wrong to lend money to a Jew.

- It *is* wrong to demand interest on a loan to a Jew.

- It *is* wrong to enslave a fellow Jew.

Nehemiah got angry because the people knowingly ignored and disobeyed God's Word. His righteous indignation was appropriate.

SOLVING THE DILEMMA

Now look at the next verse. I love this: "I consulted with myself" (Nehemiah 5:7). Aren't you glad that's in there? Yes, he got mad, but he thought before he spoke. In those moments of self-consultation, God was able to speak to Nehemiah about what to say next. Self-control is a virtue the leader cannot afford to be without.

Nehemiah, when very angry, found a way to cool down. He consulted with himself and listened to God's voice. The Hebrew word for *consult*, as used here, means "to give one self-advice, to counsel oneself." That's the very best thing to do when you get mad. You need to have a quiet place where you can lay all the emotions of your soul before God. Nobody hears but God. Marvelous therapy comes from sharing with God the hurt and the anger as you "consult with yourself," before you face the situation head-on.

Once he considered the issue and isolated the root cause, he wasted no time addressing it: "I . . . contended with the nobles and the rulers . . ." (Nehemiah 5:7).

I appreciate the fact that Nehemiah didn't penalize everybody. He approached only those who were responsible. Nehemiah called before him the guys with the heavy wallets. He lined them up in front of him and confronted them with the fact of their violations:

- You are charging interest to fellow Jews (see Nehemiah 5:7). That is wrong.

- You are enforcing the permanent slavery of the Jews (see Nehemiah 5:8). That's also wrong.

- You are losing your distinction in the eyes of the surrounding nations (see Nehemiah 5:9). That is tragic!

"You guys are over here making a bundle," Nehemiah's words implied, "and those guys (the Gentiles) across the way are looking on, saying, 'They're just like everybody else—no different at all; in fact, the whole project is a joke.'" Nothing could have thrilled Sanballat and his crowd any more than to see the job stopped because of internal strife.

After Nehemiah rebuked the ruling elite, notice their response: "Then they were silent and could not find a word to say" (Nehemiah 5:8). That is the very best response when you are under deep conviction.

A good leader, however, does not stop with rebuke. Nehemiah took steps to correct the problem—steps we should take first as leaders when we are wrong, and steps we should require of those in our organization when they blow it.

1. *Determine to stop it.* Look at verse 10: "Please, let us leave off this usury [unreasonable interest]." People occasionally ask me what they should do when convicted of sin. The answer is simple: Stop! Exercise your God-given will to eliminate the wrongdoing, right now. You cannot gradually stop sinning.

2. *Make specific plans to correct the situation as quickly as possible.* Nehemiah confronted the bankers (and asked for immediate action: "this very day"):

> Please, give back to them this very day their fields, their vineyards, their olive groves and their houses, also the hundredth part of the money [the interest] and of the grain, the new wine and the oil that you are exacting from them. (Nehemiah 5:11)

True repentance for wrong always inspires a desire to provide restitution. This is not an attempt to buy forgiveness or to throw money at a moral problem. It's a sincere desire to reverse—as much as possible—the damage one has caused.

3. *Declare your plans for correction in a promise before God.* Nehemiah moved quickly to seal the decision before the loss of money could change any minds: "So I called the priests and took an oath from them that they would do according to this promise" (Nehemiah 5:12). Nehemiah knew human nature and how to settle an issue!

4. *Realize the serious nature of your vow to God.* The Jewish people took vows very seriously. Unlike false religions, they had experience with a real God, who would hold them to their promises. Nehemiah chose to be dramatic as he reminded the people that the Lord would be watching.

> I also shook out the front of my garment and said, "Thus may God shake out every man from his house and from his possessions who does not fulfill this promise; even thus may he be shaken out and emptied." (Nehemiah 5:13)

If there's ever a time to take God seriously, it's when we make a promise to Him.

A high school buddy of mine in east Houston was just as mean and coarse and stubborn as a boy could be. On the football field, he was a fullback on offense and middle linebacker on defense. In life, he was reckless, rebellious, and tough as a boot.

He owned a speedboat and loved to zing around the shores of Galveston at top throttle, often in the middle of the night. Late one dark night, going at full speed, he hit a shallow reef and flipped the boat. He clung to a barnacled rock as the boat sank and a storm blew in. The waves pitched up and down, buffeting him against those razor-like barnacles for several hours. As blood from his wounded body spread out into the water, it occurred to him that sharks might be drawn to him—a terrifying thought. He fervently prayed, "Oh, God, if You will please deliver me from this, I'll serve You for the rest of my life. I'll make my life right. I'll do anything!" He vowed, "I'll even be a preacher" (the ultimate sacrifice, he felt). God, in His marvelous grace, dispatched the Coast Guard, and they picked him up.

A week later he had forgotten all about his vow. His body eventually healed, and he was back at his old tricks again. He later told me that every time he took his shirt off, the scars that stretched across his chest and abdomen recalled his promise to God. He did his best to put them out of mind. After every shower, he'd quickly turn his back to the mirror as he toweled off. Those scars haunted him, each one whispering, "You made a promise to God."

Several months later, my friend nearly lost his life in a head-on collision and now bears a terrible scar across his face and neck. He lost partial use of one arm and damaged some of his organs. But he lived. And he made good on his promise. He became a preacher of the gospel . . . scars and all. He says, "Every time I shave, I'm reminded that God takes promises made to Him seriously, and so should we." A vow is nothing to shrug off.

In the end, once the people came to terms with God's Word, corrected their actions, and committed their decision to the Lord, they were able to praise Him (Nehemiah 5:13). *Shalom* returned, along with the sounds of construction and God's special favor.

But What about Today?

How can we put all of this to work for us today? Let me offer four fundamental truths that not only apply to financial integrity, but also to any situation in which you or your organization have gotten off track.

First, *God is pleased when we handle our money wisely.*

Many Christians have the public aspects of leadership down pat, but their handling of money is a reproach to the name of Christ. We can clearly see from Nehemiah's experience that proper money management is important to God. How we earn it, save it, invest it, spend it, and, of course, how (or whether) we give it away.

I'm amazed that any believer thinks he or she can live without a well-thought-through plan for the use of his or her money. And no plan is complete unless it involves putting a portion of the resources God gave us back into circulation in His work. Wise handling of our savings, our investing, our spending, and our giving pleases Him and benefits everyone, including us.

Second, *prolonged personal sin takes a heavy toll on God's work in your life.* This excludes no one. Dr. Clarence Macartney, a well-known pastor for many years in Pittsburgh, addressed this issue as it relates to the pastor's responsibility to live obediently before the Lord:

> The better the man, the better the preacher. When he kneels by the bed of the dying or when he mounts the pulpit stairs, then every self-denial he has made, every Christian forbearance he has shown, every resistance to sin and temptation, will come back to him to strengthen his arm and give conviction to his voice. Likewise every evasion of duty, every indulgence of self, every compromise with evil, every unworthy thought, word, or deed, will be there at the head of the pulpit stairs to meet the minister on Sunday morning, to take the light from his eye, the power from his blow, the ring from his voice, and the joy from his heart.[1]

What's true for the pastor is also true for any believer who puts on the mantle of leadership. Sin follows you around like a shadow. If there's sin in your life, get rid of it! Lay it out before God, or get out of leadership! Be man or woman enough to step aside until you are a clean vessel. Because you're a leader, countless lives could be affected by your failure.

By the way, go back and search the first thirteen verses of Nehemiah 5. You will find no mention of any construction of the wall. Until the moral house was cleaned, no progress could be made.

Third, *correcting any problem begins by facing it head-on.* Some of us are pros at avoiding the truth. Dodging sin is far less painful than facing it. In essence, we don't want to endure the pain of reality—and so we hide behind the famous cop-out: "Oh well, nobody's perfect. You know, that's just the way I am. Always have been—always will be." Who says? God is a specialist in the business of changing lives. Claim the power of the indwelling Holy Spirit and say, "God, take over. Change my attitude. I'm sick of this habit. It is sin."

"Well, you know, I'm given to being angry. I just get mad easily. My dad had a temper; so do I."

Take care of it! Come to severe terms with that sin!

"Well, I'm given to drink. You know how it is. Man, I have trouble. I go on a binge about every third weekend."

Deal with it! Do whatever it takes to correct it.

"I'm given to gossip. It's always been hard for me to control my tongue. But that's the way I am. But so are a lot of people. Just a little problem I live with."

It's sin! Painful and long and expensive as the process may be, you cannot afford to skirt the issue any longer. Face it head-on.

Fourth, *correction is carried out most effectively when we seal it with a promise, and preferably in public.* Confess your wrong to someone who knows you well and share how you plan to deal with it, or—if God leads you—publicly share your problem and solution with your discipleship group or close circle of friends. One major step toward the correction of wrong in our lives is being accountable to a close personal friend. Or, make your vow to God known to your family. Nail it down. Lay it before someone. If you don't, Operation Erosion will set in.

Recently a very close friend and colleague purchased what he and his wife hoped would be their last home. When the job was finished, he went through the normal procedure of inspecting the work and completing a punch list. A number of workmanship issues were resolved satisfactorily, and he found nothing major. He and his wife signed the final documents and settled into their new home.

Within a few weeks, doors and windows began to stick. Then cracks appeared in the tile and walls—far more and much larger than normal settling would produce. The house deteriorated at a startling pace. Something was very wrong.

My friend hired an engineer to study the problem and his investigation uncovered a terrible secret. Old topographical maps revealed that the house had been constructed over a ravine. The developer had filled it in but, apparently, water continues to run beneath the house, carrying minute amounts of soil with it. Everything looked perfectly fine while, deep down, the earth eroded away. Eventually, the strain on the slab proved to be too much and it cracked with devastating results. The house could not be repaired or sold. It was a complete loss.

As I reflect on my friend's nightmare, it occurs to me that a similar erosion process affected not only the life of Saul, Solomon, and others in Scripture, but also the lives of people today. F. B. Meyer once said, "No man suddenly becomes base." It's always a slow, quiet process of erosion deep beneath the surface where no one notices.

Perhaps you are involved right now in the beginning of foundational cracks. The windows of finance in your life don't close as well as they used to. The doors of discipline stick. The floor of integrity is starting to pull apart in places. Rationalizing the truth and ignoring painful realities seems easer than facing them. Don't be fooled. Putty and spackle won't solve the problem.

There's a better way. It calls for absolute honesty and a refusal to excuse or ignore reality any longer. It means being sensitive and obedient to the Father's instructions. It requires personal appropriation of those things mentioned in the last part of this chapter.

My strong advice? Start today.

EIGHT

How to Handle a Promotion

Adversity is a harsh teacher. Who hasn't felt its painful lessons? It can be the frustration of unhappy employment or the disappointment of losing a job. It can suddenly reduce your status, force you to sell your home, or make you start over in another occupation that has no frills or thrills. Even worse, adversity can mean having to stand in line to apply for unemployment.

In many areas of the country, the computer industry once provided many thousands of people a taste of "the good life." The dotcoms and telecoms enjoyed an endless supply of investors, who poured multiple millions into countless enterprises. For a while, it looked as though we were going to program our way into utopia. Unfortunately, the program was flawed and when it crashed, "the good life" became pretty miserable.

Almost overnight, companies with assets in the millions were liquidated for as little as ten cents on the dollar. Investors were left empty-handed. Highly educated, uniquely skilled men and women suddenly found themselves demoted or unemployed, disillusioned, robbed of all motivation and hope. Some are still struggling to find work; most have given up and retooled for another career.

But there's a test that's even more challenging than adversity: *advancement*. That sounds wrong, but it's true! As Thomas Carlyle, the Scottish essayist and historian, once declared, "Adversity is sometimes hard upon a man; but for one man who can stand prosperity, there are a hundred that will stand adversity."[1] Few people can live in the lap of luxury and maintain their spiritual, emotional, and moral equilibrium. Sudden elevation often disturbs balance, which leads to pride and a sense of self-sufficiency—and then, a fall. It's ironic, but more of us can survive a demotion with our integrity intact better than we can a promotion. And it is at this level a godly leader shows himself or herself strong. The right kind of leaders, when promoted, know how to handle the honor.

A fellow named Asaph was the type of man Carlyle described—"one in a hundred." We don't know much about him except that he wrote twelve of the Bible's psalms. One of the twelve—Psalm 75—convinces me that Asaph had his head and heart together. Sandwiched between the first and last sections of the psalm, three verses (5–7) flash like a neon sign, announcing wise counsel for anyone with a new promotion:

> Do not lift up your horn on high,
> Do not speak with insolent pride.
> For not from the east, nor from the west,
> Nor from the desert comes exaltation;
> But God is the Judge;
> He puts down one and exalts another. (Psalms 75:5–7)

Asaph wrote something like this: "Don't toot your own horn! Remember, your promotion didn't just evolve. Behind your recent exaltation was the sovereign hand of God. You are the recipient of His goodness and grace."

How easy to forget! And your non-Christian friends won't see it like that, believe me. To them, a promotion comes by being in the right place at the right time, by knowing the right person, by shaking the right hands, by favoring the right boss, by scratching the right back. That's just not so. God is the One who suddenly lifted Joseph from an Egyptian dungeon to the role of prime minister. Almost overnight He exalted Daniel from a Babylonian boot camp to the king's right hand. He's the One who promoted Amos, an ignorant fig picker, to the polished, sophisticated halls of Bethel to be His personal spokesman. God knew that Joseph, Daniel, and Amos could handle a promotion.

And so could Nehemiah. Nehemiah provides one of the best biblical illustrations on how to handle a promotion. We've already seen how balanced he was. He worked to handle situations when things were bad, and he stood firm when things were good. Nehemiah rolled on when the project was moving ahead; and he paused and relaxed when the project briefly came to a halt. He knew when to requisition more bricks. He was a competent leader, and as a result, he was promoted.

THE ART OF ACCEPTANCE

Nehemiah writes:

> From the day that I was appointed to be their governor in the land of Judah, from the twentieth year to the thirty-second year of King Artaxerxes. . . . (Nehemiah 5:14)

Nehemiah's reaction to his appointment (and governor was the *highest* position possible) can be stated simply. In a word: *acceptance.* Many Christians seem afraid to accept responsibilities that are beyond themselves. For example, how many Christians can you name in places of political or corporate power who stand firm as uncompromising believers? The world is not short on qualified believers. Some of the most qualified people I know are born-again. But frequently we Christians adopt the idea that to be spiritual one must hide in the shadows, and that you must be unscrupulous or unkind in order to succeed as a leader. Not so!

We all need to be more like Jabez, a little-known fellow whose story is buried in a genealogical list in another book of the Old Testament. He had the courage to pray:

Oh that You would bless me indeed and enlarge my border, and that Your hand might be with me, and that You would keep me from harm that it may not pain me!" (1 Chronicles 4:10)

In other words, Jabez did not say, "Lord, give me some tiny spot where I can spend the rest of my days in obscurity." No, he looked to God and said he was willing to accept "enlarged borders." We need to believe that God wants to use us in "stretching" experiences.

If you tend to set your goals far lower than God does, you need the encouragement of Proverbs 29:2:

When the righteous increase, the people rejoice,
But when a wicked man rules, people groan.

"When the righteous increase . . ." The Hebrew word for increase means "to be made great"; a synonym would be "promoted." So, Proverbs 29:2 might be read:

> When the righteous are promoted, the people rejoice,
> But when a wicked man rules, the people groan.

Regardless of the perils of leadership and promotion, I hope you will never forget Proverbs 29:2. In this proverb, Solomon gave us a tremendous truth. When born-again people are promoted to places of increased leadership in their companies, they will have underneath them individuals who rejoice because of their "righteous" rule. How much better this is than to have the wicked promoted, who would bring with them all the tentacles of corruption and compromise.

Nehemiah accepted his appointment. Our prayer should be that God will raise up more Christians in strategic spots: college professors, university presidents, business executives, filmmakers, artists, governors, senators, and others who can fashion and frame the minds of the public. There are already some Christians in these roles, but not nearly enough.

Nehemiah accepted the governorship and immediately faced four major concerns that confront anyone who receives a promotion. All four can be found between verses 14 and 18 of chapter 5.

PROMOTIONS BRING PRIVILEGES

First, *every promotion brings privileges.* Increased responsibility always affords the recipient new or added rights, benefits, and special favors.

The wise leader will use them without abusing them. Nehemiah said that for those twelve years "neither I nor my kinsmen have eaten the governor's food allowance" (Nehemiah 5:14). As governor, he could entertain other officials with a food allowance, which worked much like an executive's expense account. Abuse on a reasonably small scale was considered a perquisite. Nevertheless, he took no liberties with this allowance so he could retain his integrity. The food was at his fingertips, but he never lost control.

How does this relate to the practicalities of today? Suppose you have been promoted in your company. With your promotion may have come the privilege of an unlimited expense account. A child of God, who is a person of integrity, will guard against taking advantage of that privilege.

The private life of the promoted leader is under the constant attack of the devil. Many individuals moving from one economic stratum to the next have been given the privilege of increased privacy. But many of these same people have floundered in their new freedom and taken a moral tumble. One time when I mentioned this problem in one of my sermons, a successful business executive came to me after the service and said, "Chuck, I want to tell you something. Before my promotion I would have never believed it, but now I recognize how easy it is to fall into the trap of moral compromise. I'm living with it constantly—the attack on my moral integrity." He gave me an illustration. Not long ago on a flight from San Francisco to Los Angeles, he encountered a most appealing temptation, and it came with a perfect built-in excuse for getting involved. After a time of struggling, he refused to yield. He told me, "I live continually with that kind of temptation. I never had such opportunities before my recent promotion. It's easier now that my company trusts me with so much more privacy."

Let me name another temptation that can come with promotion: the temptation to build one's own empire. It's significant that Nehemiah never tried to turn the power of his position into an opportunity to secure personal power. He could have become the wealthiest man in Jerusalem by purchasing land, financing private enterprises, even demanding protection money from the nobles. Nehemiah viewed this appointment as governor as a trusted position, and he closely guarded the confidence of his leaders. He refused to exploit the privileges entrusted to him.

A young man named Absalom illustrates how *not* to handle a promotion. He was the handsome son of King David. He had long, flowing black hair, and not a single blemish from the top of his head to the soles of his feet. His winsome, magnetic personality won the admiration and support of people very quickly. Externally, he exuded warmth and charisma, but in his chest beat a rebel heart. Beware a charming man or woman. I call him "the rebel prince charming."

In my study of Absalom's life, I find that David failed to train him properly. David was uninvolved as a father, leaving his family to tend itself, usually with tragic results. Perhaps due to guilt over his negligence, David promoted his son to the court. That was a major mistake. Absalom stole the hearts of the people by setting up his own court just outside the palace. As he ruled on cases, he reminded the people that they obtained justice from him that could not have been gained from his father. Eventually, he garnered enough political clout and military power to overthrow the government and drive his own father off the throne and out of the city.

Individuals with increased responsibilities must face the temptations that come with privilege. They are but one of the reasons that

Carlyle said for every hundred who can live with adversity, only one can handle prosperity.

PROMOTIONS THREATEN POLICIES

When you receive a promotion, expect to face the complications of your predecessor's policies, both good and bad. In the case of a well-liked former boss, the organization will quote him as though he were a saint, which can bring terrible pressure on the new person. Even in the case of a cruel, corrupt former boss, the people he ruled over tend to resist change. They don't know you and they are likely to cling to what was bad, for fear that it might become worse. This was Nehemiah's challenge. His administration replaced a corrupt government. The people were used to dirty politics—including overtaxation, extortion, and favoritism:

> But the former governors who were before me laid burdens on
> the people and took from them bread and wine besides forty
> shekels of silver; even their servants domineered the people.
> (Nehemiah 5:15)

Nehemiah came into office and his counselors probably said something like, "You know, Nehemiah, politics work a little different here than you're used to back in Susa, where you have the benefit of laws and a strong security force. Here, they have a system that seems to work for them and it's been this way for a long time."

"Oh? What have they been doing?"

"Well, they get a little extra money from increased taxes here and there. After all, you need to look the part, or people won't respect you. And if you have some buddies who need a job . . . Well, that way, you can be sure that your administration remains loyal. Nobody will squawk. It's part of the system."

Take note of his answer in the latter part of the verse. "I did not do so because of the fear of God." He said in effect, "I have a job to do, the God of heaven promoted me to do it, and I answer to Him. He will protect me, so I have no need to continue the corruption."

Shortly after I started teaching the leadership principles I found in Nehemiah, an executive came to see me. He and his wife were amazed by the relevance of the book. Before all this, he had been promoted to a new position with his company and quickly discovered that the policies of his predecessor were both unfair and illegal. As he began to reform the system, he faced considerable backlash. His life was threatened more than once, and he and his wife received numerous obscene telephone calls. Ugly, untrue rumors about him began to circulate. He became a hated man because he dismantled the unethical policies that stood for so long.

He endured and successfully cleaned up the mess. When he accepted another promotion with even a greater measure of authority, he left a respectable operation behind. Predictably, the new position had its own set of policies that needed correction—even more than the last.

This is not unusual. Every person in government, every executive, and every military leader has to wrestle with policies. They constantly hear, "We've always done it this way," or "We've never done it that way before." The leader's integrity is at stake, which is why few people can handle the pressures of leadership without compromising their integrity.

Despite the pressure to fold, Nehemiah stood firm. He knew he had a choice. He could bear the pressure alone and let it come between himself and God, or he could allow the Lord to bear the load. By answering only to God, the stress became the catalyst that fused his heart to the Lord's and sealed his integrity.

Nehemiah never abused the privileges, even refusing to make full use of what was rightfully his to enjoy. And he reformed the policies rather than perpetuate corruption, even if it meant weakening his position by human standards. In fact, he drove hard in the opposite direction.

> I also applied myself to the work on this wall; we did not buy any land, and all my servants were gathered there for the work. (Nehemiah 5:16)

What a rare man! That's what I call genuine leadership.

PROMOTIONS INVOLVE PROJECTS

The third area of concern to a new position of leadership is the slate of projects. *Every promotion comes with a set of projects that must be completed.* Nehemiah did not accept the position of governor so he could engage in his own pet enterprises. He stayed at the task of building the wall. He did not abuse the promotion. He didn't turn it into a lucrative opportunity for himself. He never lost sight of the goal. Nor did he get sidetracked from the major objective: constructing the wall.

You might think, "Well, Nehemiah didn't have many problems

because he wasn't really very well-known. And besides, he had the political support of people like Artaxerxes." If you are questioning the visibility of his position, take a close look at Nehemiah 5:17–18:

> Moreover, there were at my table one hundred and fifty Jews and officials, besides those who came to us from the nations that were around us. Now that which was prepared for each day was one ox and six choice sheep, also birds were prepared for me; and once in ten days all sorts of wine were furnished in abundance. Yet for all this I did not demand the governor's food allowance, because the servitude was heavy on this people. (Nehemiah 5:17–18)

The fire in the kitchen never went out. He had to feed thousands of people every month. That's a lot of groceries! Nehemiah was a well-known, highly sought-after political figure, a very public man. High ranking public officials from surrounding nations were his dinner guests. But Nehemiah never lost sight of the project. His belly didn't block his vision. He maintained a sharp eye that refused to be dulled by people coming and going. Some leaders can do that. Many can't.

Solomon couldn't when he became the richest man in the world. In fact, from one importing enterprise alone, according to 1 Kings 10:14, Solomon made the equivalent of $876 million annually (based on the price of gold at the time of publication). He owned hand-crafted shields containing enough gold to be worth a total of $64 million. Scripture tells us that under Solomon's leadership the silver in Jerusalem became as common as stones. But he couldn't handle the pressures of responsibility. He lost sight of his primary responsibilities. Listen to this eloquent yet tragic analysis by G. Frederick Owen:

Maddened with the love of show, Solomon swung into a fever-
ish career of wastefulness, impropriety, and oppression. Not satisfied with the necessary buildings and legitimate progress of his
past years, he over-burdened his people with taxation, enslaved
some, and ruthlessly instigated the murder of others.

All Solomon's drinking vessels were of gold, and those of his
house were of pure gold. The shields of his mighty men were made
of beaten gold, and his great throne was made of ivory and overlaid
with the finest gold. . . . Solomon, like many another absolute
monarch, drove too fast and traveled too far. . . . The monarch
became debauched and effeminate; an egotist and cynic, so satiated
with the sensual and material affairs of life that he became skepti-
cal of all good—to him, all became "vanity and vexation of spirit."[2]

Solomon couldn't handle his promotion. Over the long haul, the
fiber of his life began to come apart under the stress of temptation.
Ironically, he stared into the sunlight of God's limitless blessings and
became blinded to his rightful role and calling.

PROMOTIONS AFFECT PEOPLE

Finally, Nehemiah's advancement affected the lives of others. You
have no leader if you have no people. *Leading is a people-oriented job.*
Nehemiah 5:18 says:

Yet for all this [the abundance of food] I did not demand the
governor's food allowance, because the servitude was heavy on
this people. (Nehemiah 5:18)

Frequently, a strong leader will become so focused on the objective that he or she runs roughshod over the people who work to achieve it. Nehemiah never neglected his project, but he also kept the needs of the people in clear focus. He led with compassion. That doesn't mean that he allowed his emotions to dictate policy, but he allowed his concern for the people to influence how he carried them out. Upon seeing that the people were overburdened and overtaxed, he backed off and said, "Let's progress at a reasonable pace. Let's keep in step with one another, and face one problem at a time." One leader put it like this: "The man who is impatient with weakness will be defective in his leadership. The evidence of our strength lies not in streaking ahead but in a willingness to adapt our stride to the slower pace of our weaker brethren, while not forfeiting our lead. If we run too far ahead, we lose our power to influence."[3]

That's good advice for a strong leader. Nehemiah never lost his sensitive spirit.

Nehemiah's heart reveals itself beautifully in this passage concerning his promotion. Two phrases in particular demonstrate how he was able to endure the temptations of increased privileges, overcome the backward momentum of longstanding policies, maintain his focus on the project, and care for the needs of people. The first phrase appears in verse 15: "I did not do so because of the fear of God."

Nehemiah nurtured a relationship with the Lord that stood stronger than any of those external forces. In spite of his salary, the privileges, the policies, or the pressure, he said, in effect, "My accountability to my Lord is the focus of my life. I fear Him too much to indulge myself."

That doesn't mean that people rightly related to God can't have nice things. However, we are not to allow nice things to have us. Let's hold everything loosely so that God can remove from our grasp whatever He chooses to take from us.

Verse 19 contains the second phrase that reveals Nehemiah's heart: "Remember me, O my God, for good, according to all that I have done for this people." This could appear to be a bold, self-promoting prayer at first glance, asking to be rewarded for all the good he's doing for the people of Jerusalem. But it's much more. This is a prayer that invites the Lord to hold him accountable for his actions and to treat him accordingly. In essence, he joins the psalmist, who wrote:

> Search me, O God, and know my heart;
> Try me and know my anxious thoughts;
> And see if there be any hurtful way in me,
> And lead me in the everlasting way. (Psalms 139:23–24)

Furthermore, he commits himself to such conduct as would be worthy of reward.

Being demoted would be tough to endure, but surviving the perils of a promotion is even tougher! Adversity forces us to trust, to wait on God, to turn to Him for strength. But advancement can bring a host of difficulties: pride, temptation to abuse privileges, pressure from former policies, distraction from the basic objectives, and an inclination to overlook the needs of people who are under our authority.

Small wonder that Carlyle suggested that only one in a hundred could pass the test of prosperity!

Nehemiah passed the test and we admire him for it.

The question is, will you?

NINE

Operation Intimidation

The early seventies was an interesting time for professional football. It was after the days when top players, such as Johnny Unitas, had to beg for $7,000 a year and supplement their income with part-time work, but before free agency made multi-million dollar contracts a common occurrence. The game's popularity was just then growing to include more than just the hard-core sports enthusiast; it was becoming the topic around every water cooler in the United States each Monday morning.

It was during this time that George Allen moved to Washington DC to become the head coach of the Redskins and, like the politicians that populated the nation's capital, he promised everybody the moon. He told them he would transform the Redskins into a championship football team within just a few months. He even promised the Super Bowl by the second season.

The team had a successful preseason that first year. Then, early in the regular season, they won several amazing victories. It appeared the Redskins were to be lifted from their familiar role of loser to the uncommon role of winner. Yet, the past eventually caught up with them. They began to lose and lose and lose. But the blame fell, at least in part, not on Coach George Allen, but on their quarterback Sonny Jurgenson, who, in my opinion, was one of the most colorful and effective quarterbacks ever to play the game. Jurgenson possessed a quality I deeply admire: personal security. Nothing seemed to intimidate him.

One Sunday evening after another defeat, Sonny was getting ready to take a shower and go home. A sportswriter leaned over to him in the locker room and said, "Say, Sonny, be honest now. Don't all these off-the-wall remarks we write and all this public flak disturb you? Doesn't it make you want to quit when people throw things at you from the stands and when you get those dirty letters?"

Sonny just leaned back, gave a big, toothless grin, and sighed, "Naw . . . not really. I don't want to quit. I've been in this game long enough to know that every quarterback, every week of the season, spends his time either in the penthouse or in the outhouse." Sonny's comment highlights an important fact. If you are a leader, you spend your time either on the top or on the bottom. You're either hero or villain; respected or reviled. Rarely anything between those extremes. People in leadership must live on the yo-yo of public opinion: the target for cheap shots on the bottom, the object of great admiration on the upside. The outhouse is difficult to endure. But it's when we are under the verbal attack of the intimidating public that we show our true colors.

I have discovered, after a number of years in the ministry, that this is true even in the spiritual realm. You commit yourself to a life of faith, you declare before God and man that you are going to walk with Him regardless, and suddenly, it happens! The enemy turns every gun he can upon you to blast you out of the saddle, to make you finish your season in defeat, to have you think that it's really not worth it after all.

A Well-timed Attack

Nehemiah, as reported in chapter 6, was not in the penthouse. Even though he had been a faithful, stable, and consistent leader, a plot to defeat him was underway. The attack upon Nehemiah was very significant because it happened at a crucial juncture in his life. Verse 1 tells us the attack occurred when he was nearly finished with the greatest task that Jerusalem's citizens had seen in their generation. Not very long before they were ready to cut the ribbon and enjoy a jubilant celebration, the enemy began to plot Nehemiah's demise.

That is so true to life today that I can hardly believe it! This must be one of the reasons God says to the proud person to "take heed lest he fall" (1 Corinthians 10:12). So often the vulnerable person isn't the one who stumbles, but the one who thinks he isn't capable of falling.

In Scripture, such failures occurred time and again. When did Bathsheba cross the gaze of David? At a time when he had not known defeat in battle. From the time he took the kingdom until he fell with Bathsheba, David had not known defeat—politically, militarily, or personally. When did Jonah fall into self-pity? After the greatest revival that had ever swept a city. When did Joseph receive that temptation from Mrs. Potiphar? Soon after he had been promoted under Mr. Potiphar's leadership and given free run of the house.

Frankly, some of my most discouraging times occur on Mondays. I can't explain why. After a great Sunday, when we've been uplifted in one service after another; when we've heard testimonies and words of encouragement; when we've sung, had fellowship, worshiped and really enjoyed the Lord together, I sink into discouragement come Monday. I've also found when I am approaching a tremendous, mountaintop experience, I tend to hit a slump. Maybe you have experienced this.

A Subtle Strategy

Nehemiah was already planning the dedication service for the completed wall when the enemy attacked. Verse 2, through the end of the sixth chapter, tells us the story of these subtle attacks. There were three different kinds, each prompted by the enemy's motive to stop the project by deterring Nehemiah and his men through discouragement. God permitted these tests to strengthen His servant.

The Lord never wants our dedication or integrity softened by extended ease and irresponsible luxury. That's unrealistic. That's penthouse living. Every once in a while we are allowed to enjoy seasons of abundance, but not at the expense of our relationship with Him. And that fact can be difficult to accept. G. K. Chesterton put it this way: "The Christian ideal has not been tried and found wanting. It has been found difficult; and left untried."[1]

While this kind of life is not for weaklings, Nehemiah committed himself to God's way. Then came the attack. It first came in the form of a polite invitation, which on the surface appeared to be quite harmless. In fact, it sounded like something he ought to accept.

Sanballat and Geshem sent a message to me, saying, "Come, let us meet together at Chephirim in the plain of Ono." (Nehemiah 6:2)

The word "together" suggests a desire for an amicable visit. The plain of Ono was located about twenty miles north of Jerusalem, and it was a beautiful, verdant valley. Sanballat and Geshem were saying, in effect, "You need to get away for a while. You've been laying bricks too long, Nehemiah. We've had our spats, a few little disagreements, but let's get together. Come on up to Ono."

Nehemiah said, "Oh, no!" to Ono. Somehow, he knew their motives were not what they seemed. He writes, "They were planning to harm me" (Nehemiah 6:2). I can't explain how any leader in God's family can be gifted with this sixth sense from above. He gets to the edge of danger and something inside says, "I don't dare get into that; there's something wrong."

That doesn't mean we should live the life of an isolationist; it does mean we should live a life of discernment. Discernment is a God-given quality a leader must possess. Discernment allows you to read between the lines. In this invitation Nehemiah sensed trouble. He probably said to himself, "If I get up there in that place, I might be kidnapped or even murdered. I know for sure that as soon as I leave, the work here will suffer."

But they were planning to harm me. So I sent messengers to them saying, "I am doing a great work and I cannot come down. Why should the work stop while I leave it and come down to you?" (Nehemiah 6:2–3)

To put it another way, there's a great difference between being an available man or woman of God and being a puppet of people—a great difference. Some people never understand how you can say no. But every leader must reserve that right. One of the marks of maturity is the ability to say no without explanation.

Nevertheless, his enemies didn't give up: "They sent messages to me four times" (Nehemiah 6:4). Perhaps they sent nice little embossed invitations with lovely printing, each one with a note at the bottom: *Request No. 2, Request No. 3, Final Request.* But each time Nehemiah held his ground. "I answered them in the same way" (Nehemiah 6:4).

What a secure man! *Unintimidated* is the word. But he was about to face another pressure tactic: "Then Sanballat sent his servant to me in the same manner a fifth time with an open letter in his hand" (Nehemiah 6:5).

First, there had been the personal requests. Now here was an open letter. His enemies had taken the pressure to the next level, from private invitation to public petition. No longer was it a private letter in a personal envelope; this time a messenger came and opened it for everyone to read. Notice the intimidating, threatening remarks of this open letter:

It is reported among the nations, and Gashmu says, that you and the Jews are planning to rebel; therefore you are rebuilding the wall. And you are to be their king, according to these reports. You have also appointed prophets to proclaim in Jerusalem concerning you, "A king is in Judah!" And now it will be reported to the king according to these reports. So come now, let us take counsel together. (Nehemiah 6:6–7)

Allow me to elaborate on their tactics, reading between the lines: "You wouldn't come when we sent our invitation, and so we're letting the truth be known. We plan to expose you. We want everybody to know two things. First, when you came to Jerusalem, you had an evil motive. It was not just to rebuild the wall. You came for the express purpose of collecting a group of people around you so you could lead a revolution. Furthermore, your method is evil. You want to be the king and so you're spreading the prophets throughout the land to proclaim that Nehemiah will be the king, not Artaxerxes. So we're going to send the word back to the king in Persia. If you don't want this complication, you'd better visit with us." This is intimidation, plain and simple.

THE RUMOR MILL

Sanballat's weapon of choice here is *rumor*, which has at least two distinctive characteristics. First, *a source is never declared.* Note the vague reference, "It is reported among the nations . . ." This lends an air of credence to both the story and the storyteller. It suggests that the story is widely reported and, therefore, credible, and that the storyteller is more in touch with the masses who hold this "truth." This can be very intimidating because Sanballat appears to speak for a majority, and if the matter were to be investigated by Artaxerxes, he would side against Nehemiah.

Second, rumors usually involve *exaggeration* and *inaccuracy.* A rumor builds upon a kernel of truth, which gives gullible people—or people with a motive—just enough reason to swallow the lie whole. Then it's passed from person to person as the exaggeration compounds itself, almost like magic.

Have you ever played the party game "Gossip"? The first person in a line of ten people whispers something to the person standing next to him. He or she whispers it quickly to the next one, and on it goes down the line. By the time it gets to person number ten, the message is garbled beyond belief. And that's with only ten people—who are trying to cooperate!

Rumors in the wild perpetuate and mutate at a much more dangerous rate, usually fueled by fear. "Did you hear about Nehemiah? He's built the wall, now he's raising an army and calling himself king! If we don't do something, Artaxerxes will be down here in a flash and wipe us off the map—all of us!"

Furthermore, rumors lead to deep personal hurt and misunderstanding. What was the result of this report concerning Nehemiah? It hurt him—in fact it was *designed to hurt.*

Nehemiah found himself on the horns of a dilemma. If he refused to go to Ono, it would be tantamount to saying, "I'm afraid to let the truth be known." But if he went to Ono, he would leave the work on the wall and would play into the hands of the enemy. He would likely be killed, which would permanently end the work on the wall. This was a classic no-win situation.

People who spread rumors invariably lack wisdom. Discernment causes a person to ask such searching questions as, "Is it necessary to say this? Is this confidential information? Is it even true? Do I have any right to pass this on?" Wisdom prompts the reply, "Don't open your mouth because God hates those who sow discord among His people." (Of the seven things God hates, three relate to the tongue. See Proverbs 6:16–19.)

Rumormongers also lack *accurate information.* Anytime you want to find the truth, you must first find the source. Never trust information that doesn't come with the proper credentials. And if you want to watch a rumormonger drop his jaw and turn pale, ask, "Can I quote you on that?"

Further, rumor-spreaders frequently fail to choose the *proper setting* for sharing information. A wise person will ask, "Will this benefit the person who hears me?" Or better, "Can he do anything about it? Or will I be pouring useless hearsay into someone's ears?" When you give information to people who are critical and negative, knowing they can't do anything about the situation anyway, that's an unwise move. Share information only when it is relevant to the situation and useful for bringing people together.

Not every critic is an enemy of the faith, nor is every person who criticizes inherently evil. However, I'm not fully convinced that the term *critic* applies to the gossip. A person who is genuinely interested in the truth uses his tongue to secure the truth and to apply it in love.

What should be your response when you are confronted by a gossip? Frankly, I think direct confrontation is the best response. The next time someone brings gossip or rumors to your ears, gently confront him or her. Ask kindly for the source of the information and ask how it might be used for good. But beware! Gossips are a vindictive lot, and you will likely become his or her next victim. Standing for truth requires courage and inevitably comes with its share of bruises.

In the case of Nehemiah, no one in attendance could attest to the truth. He was confronted with an open letter containing accusations built upon a lie. And he responded beautifully. His approach to the problem in verse 8 would be a good model to follow if you are ever the target of gossip. First, Nehemiah calmly denied the charge: "Such things as you are saying have not been done." Second, he put the blame where it belonged: "You are inventing them in your own mind." Third, he took his case before the Lord:

> For all of them were trying to frighten us, thinking, "They will become discouraged with the work and it will not be done." But now, O God, strengthen my hands. (Nehemiah 6:9)

It is impossible for a leader—or any person, for that matter—with a sensitive spirit not to be hurt by a rumor. I don't care how strong a leader you are, you will experience times when cutting, unfair remarks dig deep. Lives and reputations have been utterly destroyed by rumor campaigns. Afterward, when you've picked up the pieces and put things back together, you must move on. Keep the damage in perspective. Remember that the Lord will make sure that the truth will win in the end.

Let me say something to those who gossip. If yours is a loose tongue, God is going to have to deal with it. You see, gossip is a major reason for disunity in the family of God and a chief contributor to the demise of organizations. If we have disagreements that must be expressed, we should take them to leaders who can do something about them, to those who will really listen, evaluate, and respond to what we have to say. If you have allowed bad-mouthing your boss to become a habit, you're wrong. You need to express your concerns to someone in authority in a calm, reasonable tone.

I believe every telephone ought to have engraved on its back Paul's words to the church in Ephesus: "Let no foul speech whatever come out of your mouth, but only what serves well to improve the occasion, so as to add blessing to the listeners" (Ephesians 4:29 MLB).[2]

Observe that the purpose of the letter to Nehemiah was to frighten him: "For all of them were trying to frighten us . . ." (Nehemiah 6:9). But Nehemiah didn't give in. He persisted in what he knew to be the will of God.

Isn't it interesting that when one approach didn't work, another approach was used? Enemies can be relentless! First, they tried to stop the project by a personal request. Second, they used the open-letter approach to halt progress. Finally, they employed a religious-sounding (yet intimidating) warning: "Run for your life!"

> When I entered the house of Shemaiah the son of Delaiah, son of Mehetabel, who was confined at home, he said, "Let us meet together in the house of God, within the temple, and let us close the doors of the temple, for they are coming to kill you, and they are coming to kill you at night." (Nehemiah 6:10)

I can't imagine the fear that Nehemiah felt. He was merely a cup-bearer who wanted to help his countrymen. Becoming an assassin's target was not what he had volunteered for. Can you picture it? Some night Nehemiah would put on his pajamas, blow out the candle, and lie down only to hear a noise outside. A contract killer stalking him? Then he received another "invitation," this time from a supposed friend. In addition to the fear of attack from Jerusalem's enemies, he also had to watch his back among his countrymen.

His enemies, both inside and outside the wall, underestimated him. They hoped to use his own fear of assassination against him in a plot to assassinate him! I love his reply:

"Should a man like me flee? And could one such as I go into the temple to save his life? I will not go in." Then I perceived that surely God had not sent him, but he uttered his prophecy against me because Tobiah and Sanballat had hired him. (Nehemiah 6:11–12)

Merriam-Webster's Dictionary defines *intimidate* as "to make timid or fearful: frighten; especially: to compel or deter by or as if by threats."

I have a pastor friend who once had a very successful ministry on the East Coast. The very first Sunday morning when he began this ministry, he found an unsigned letter on his desk. (Letters of this sort are almost always unsigned.) The neatly printed letter said: "If you do not send your children to [such and such] Christian School, you will split the church." It was signed: "A concerned member."

"Nehemiah, they're going to come in the middle of the night and they are going to get you. And if you don't get away, you've had it!" And Nehemiah replied, "I can't go."

"Why not?"

"Because God doesn't want me to go."

"Well, then, you're a fool."

"No. I'm walking by faith. God will protect me because it would be a sin for me to run and hide." Somehow, Nehemiah saw through the web of deception that threatened to entangle him.

[Shemaiah] was hired for this reason, that I might become frightened and act accordingly and sin, so that they might have an evil
report in order that they could reproach me. (Nehemiah 6:13)

I find two points of interest in Nehemiah's choice of words. First,
he considered it sin to follow Shemaiah's plan to hide out in the temple. Second, his enemies considered it sin as well. Only priests were
allowed in the temple sanctuary (see Numbers 3:10; 18:7).
Shemaiah, the son of a priest, Nehemiah, and Nehemiah's enemies
all knew that following the plan would be disobedience, a desecration of the Lord's house.

Feeling fear is not itself sin, but *yielding* to the intimidation of
God's enemies in an effort to preserve himself would display a lack
of confidence in the Lord. And if the fear were to grow strong
enough, it might even cause a good leader to blur the line between
right and wrong.

Note the reason his enemies wanted Nehemiah to sin: "so that
they might have an evil report in order that they could reproach me."
They hoped to lure him into making their gossip a legitimate complaint. Soon nosy gossips would have been heard whispering to one
another, "Guess where Nehemiah's sleeping tonight. He says, 'Do
not be afraid of them; remember the Lord who is great and awe-
some,' and 'Our God will fight for us,' yet he's willing to desecrate
the temple to save his own hide!"

Nehemiah had just cause for his suspicion that rumors could very
easily fly if he chose to accept this clandestine meeting at the temple.
He was surrounded by people who kept the Jerusalem post office
busy! "Also in those days many letters went from the nobles of Judah

to Tobiah, and Tobiah's letters came to them" (Nehemiah 6:17).

Tobiah was the worst kind of enemy, a supposed ally whom Nehemiah's followers respected and trusted.

> For many in Judah were bound by oath to him because he was the son-in-law of Shecaniah the son of Arah, and his son Jehohanan had married the daughter of Meshullam the son of Berechiah. Moreover, they were speaking about his good deeds in my presence and reported my words to him. Then Tobiah sent letters to frighten me. (Nehemiah 6:18–19)

Though related by marriage and by blood to the Jews in the surrounding area and a trusted public figure for people inside the wall, Tobiah was Nehemiah's archenemy—an unbeliever, an interloper from Aram who somehow weaseled his way into positions of influence. He pretended be one with the Jews, and yet Tobiah "sent letters to frighten" Nehemiah.

Nehemiah never allowed the rumors and political intrigue to deter him from his mission. I don't see that he even took the time to respond unless forced to do so. He merely shrugged off the accusations, stayed at his task, focused on the needs of the people, and allowed the results to speak for him.

MISSION ACCOMPLISHED!

"So the wall was completed. . ." Such sweet, satisfying words. And what a magnificent accomplishment! Even as the attacks continued, the final bricks were laid in place. With the completion of the wall, the tables turned: "When all our enemies heard of it, and all the nations surrounding us saw it, they lost their confidence . . ." (Nehemiah 6:16).

That has to be the most thrilling experience in the world—to see God come to the rescue when you have been helpless. In the middle of the incessant assault of the enemy, in spite of the endless verbal barrage, the wall was built! Even as the enemy blasts, God builds.

We need this reminder today because it is impossible to do the will of God, to walk by faith, to pass those bricks without suffering attack by the enemy. I encourage all who read these pages to stand firm. The Lord strengthened Nehemiah through three severe attacks: (1) threatening personal letters, (2) an open letter impugning his motives and character, and (3) an attempt to paralyze him with fear. None of them worked! The wall continued to go up. Because Nehemiah and his workers were in the center of God's will, they enjoyed His special protection.

Persistence pays rich dividends. I am reminded of the words Winston Churchill once delivered to the Harrow School: "Never give in! Never, never, never, never. Never give in!" If honor is at stake, if a good principle is at stake, if you know you're accomplishing something that would please the Lord, never, *never* quit.

TEN

Revival at Water Gate?

Common to every genuine revival in history are two primary forces: the faithful proclamation of the Bible, *God's Word*, and the responsive mobilization of believers, *God's people*.

Strange as it may sound, a revival doesn't begin with the unsaved. The Lord sparks a revival by igniting the fire of His Word as He then mobilizes His people to go and win the lost. While the Lord prepares and changes hearts, He insists that His people join Him in proclaiming the truth so that we can share His joy in the victory. Let me illustrate this concept of revival from the pages of history.

Almost five centuries ago in Germany, God lit a fire in the lives of several men. As God burned His Word into the hearts of these few, it wasn't long before that flame passed to men who began to carry the torch throughout Europe: men such as Huss, Melanchthon, Calvin, Zwingli, Savonarola, and, of course, Luther.

Martin Luther reformed the church in Germany first by translating the Scriptures into the native language of the people, then by passionately preaching the Word. He taught scores of other men and women who, in turn, taught many others. Moreover, he wrote hymns that reflected the Bible's view of God, Christ, salvation, and grace. Gradually the old, dead, works-based religiosity of Romanism gave way to living, vibrant, grace-filled Christianity. The people of Germany not only read the Bible in their own language, but they also sang of their faith from a hymnal.

An old Bohemian Psalter includes a picture of John Wycliffe striking a spark, John Huss kindling the coals, and Luther brandishing the flame. It says in effect, "Reformation has come! Revival has occurred!" That Psalter is dated 1572, which proves that the people of the Reformation era understood what God was doing.

Nearly three hundred years later, the Wesley brothers, John and Charles, perpetuated the "first great awakening" in England. In his fifty years of preaching, John delivered forty thousand sermons, addressed audiences as great as twenty thousand people without the assistance of a public-address system, and traveled two hundred and twenty-five thousand miles, most of it on horseback, proclaiming the Word of God. His gifted brother, Charles, left the church a magnificent legacy of thousands of hymns. Among them were many we still love to sing:

- "And Can It Be?"
- "O for a Thousand Tongues"
- "Hark! the Herald Angels Sing"
- "Christ for the World, We Sing"
- "Arise, My Soul, Arise"
- "Jesus, Lover of My Soul"

The Reformation and the First Great Awakening are modern examples of revivals. Both began with a return to God's Word and a clear decision to preach it faithfully despite the consequences. The response was overwhelming.

THE FIRST REVIVAL

Tucked away in the old Book of Nehemiah is the first recorded revival. And of all places, the revival occurred at the Water Gate. According to Nehemiah 8:1, "All the people gathered as one man at the square which was in front of the Water Gate." This would be the setting of the most exciting experience since the completion of the wall.

It is helpful to know that at this time there was a spiritual vacuum in the city. The wall reconstruction project had been completed and the people had moved into their own dwellings. Nehemiah 7 provides a detailed description of the organizational structure, which shows that the people had become well organized, well defended, and well governed. But in this community, even though its residents had nice homes and good jobs and were well protected, they still lacked something. Nehemiah sensed the spiritual vacuum, as did the people.

This illustrates a timeless truth: *It is pointless to have a well-constructed superstructure if little or no life exists on the inside.* This is not only true in the church; the same can be said of any organization, Christian or secular. We've all experienced the steely, impersonal touch of institutional efficiency. People are not manufactured cogs that can be processed by nonthinking machines. We are highly individual, complex creatures with motives and needs that are easily violated when ignored.

Many organizations remind me of a story about an impressive machine. It had hundreds of wheels, cogs, gears, pulleys, belts, and lights, all of which moved or lit up at the touch of a button. When someone asked, "What does it do?" the inventor replied, "Oh, it doesn't do anything—but doesn't it run beautifully?"

Leaders, take note! Satisfactory buildings and a well-organized operation are essential. But getting your people grouped, protected, and relating smoothly with one another is more important than almost anything. All organizations have their "walls" to build, but an effective leader must be more concerned with what happens inside those walls.

Three factors ensured that the walls served their purpose.

1. *Fresh personnel.* Evidently, both the Lord and Nehemiah knew that Ezra would do a better job at getting things going inside that wall than Nehemiah. Here is another example of entrusting the ongoing tasks of a project to others who are more adept and better qualified than the person at the top. We have already seen how Nehemiah was good at delegating tasks. The late management guru of our day, Peter Drucker, would have been proud of him. He wrote:

> There was considerable resistance to decentralization in the forties and fifties. It was widely feared that it would weaken top management and would lead to "top management abdication."
>
> By now managers everywhere have learned that decentralization strengthens top management. It makes it more effective and more capable of doing its own tasks.[1]

Knowing this to be true, Nehemiah utilized the skills of Ezra at this crucial time in Jerusalem. And Ezra became the spokesman before the people.

2. *Established truth.* The Scripture was openly and boldly proclaimed. Often when success comes—whether in business or in the

church—there is a tendency to operate on emotional highs (enthusiasm, good feelings) instead of using the "authentic fuel" of established truth. Remember that the first major thrust in a genuine revival is the proclamation of Scripture. The apostles, who set the pace for the early church, stayed with God's Word. Even when growth occurred and vast numbers of people became followers of Christ, those who led this first-century revival never ventured from the Word of God. And the Reformation was all about a return to God's Word as the final authority and source of truth.

I find it helpful to discover in this section of Nehemiah's memoirs the characteristics of authentic Bible exposition. Beginning with the opening words of chapter 8, we read how the events transpired:

> And all the people gathered as one man at the square which was in front of the Water Gate, and they asked Ezra the scribe to bring the book of the law of Moses which the Lord had given to Israel. Then Ezra the priest brought the law before the assembly of men, women and all who could listen with understanding, on the first day of the seventh month. He read from it before the square which was in front of the Water Gate from early morning until midday, in the presence of men and women, those who could understand; and all the people were attentive to the book of the law. (Nehemiah 8:1–3)

First, *there was the reading of God's Word.* Exposition begins here—not with the opinion of man, but with the established truth of God. Second, *there was an obvious respect for the truth.* Note that the people listened attentively as they stood on their feet for hours.

Ezra opened the book in the sight of all the people for he was standing above all the people; and when he opened it, all the people stood up. Then Ezra blessed the Lord the great God. And all the people answered, "Amen, Amen!" while lifting up their hands; then they bowed low and worshiped the Lord with their faces to the ground. (Nehemiah 8:5–6)

Third, *the truth was explained so that all who heard understood.*

They read from the book, from the law of God, translating to give the sense so that they understood the reading. (Nehemiah 8:8)

After an oral reading from the book, those gifted in its truths exposited the text to make the meaning clear. The word *translating* means in Hebrew "to make something distinct, to separate it from something else so as to make it flow together in a meaningful fashion." They separated the Word, the verses, and the passages so that they fit into place in an intelligent, clear, and understandable fashion.

But why did they need to translate the Scripture? Remember, these people were Jews by birth, but not by tongue or culture. These Jews, who had come from Persia to Jerusalem, were surrounded by a Persian mentality and lifestyle. Having been reared in that environment, naturally they brought it with them.

The words read to them were from the Hebrew Bible. They heard a Hebrew Bible through Persian ears. There was a communication breakdown. And so these trained scribes took the Hebrew text and made it meaningful to the ears of the listeners. After they had translated it, the verse says, "they gave the sense." They unlocked the door leading to understanding—the ability to see something beneath the surface. They gave their audience an in-depth meaning of the words and passages so that the people could understand and a transformation in their thinking would begin.

Fourth, *the truth was applied.* Those who heard, responded. (Note the presence of the leader, Nehemiah, the governor.)

> Then Nehemiah, who was the governor, and Ezra the priest and scribe, and the Levites who taught the people said to all the people, "This day is holy to the Lord your God; do not mourn or weep." For all the people were weeping when they heard the words of the law. (Nehemiah 8:9)

The people began to weep because they knew they were guilty. They thought back over the years they had lived with no spiritual guidance. They also recalled the sins of their forefathers that had caused them to fall into captivity. The depth of their guilt brought weeping. (And that's a good sign, by the way. At times, guilt is an excellent motivation. Not all guilt is wrong. Sometimes God uses guilt to bring people out of sin and into a saving knowledge of Jesus Christ.) In this moment of guilt, Nehemiah stood and said, "Now, stop that. God is forgiving. Let's move on. This is a holy day. This is a day not to cry but to celebrate."

> He said to them, "Go, eat of the fat, drink of the sweet, and send portions to him who has nothing prepared; for this day is holy to our Lord. Do not be grieved, for the joy of the Lord is your strength." So the Levites calmed all the people, saying, "Be still, for the day is holy, do not be grieved." (Nehemiah 8:10–11)

During the 1960s, some high-profile cultural figures declared, "God is dead." To the Jews who had been in exile for seventy years, God at least seemed to have been away on a long journey; they had "lost touch" and were fearful of Him. Years ago, I saw a camper with a big sign that read, "God is back, and boy is He mad!" The Jerusalem Jews heard the reading of the Law, understood their guilt, and thought, "God's been gone, but now He's back and He's mad."

Nehemiah and his men said, in effect, "Oh, no. God didn't leave; *you* left! You should celebrate today. This marvelous God of heaven still stands with open arms and says, 'I'm ready to forgive and forget. I'll receive everyone who repents; come to Me just as you are.'"

To their credit, the people applied the message and, in doing so, they became a mobilized people:

> All the people went away to eat, to drink, to send portions and to celebrate a great festival, because they understood the words which had been made known to them. (Nehemiah 8:12)

That is the essence of a revival! The Bible had been proclaimed and the people began to mobilize. As a wise leader, Nehemiah employed fresh personnel. As a godly leader, he stayed with the established truth. But there was yet another factor that gave meaning to the building of the wall.

3. *Distinguishing between the means and the end.* This is, essentially, a distinction between long-term and short-term objectives. Nehemiah was sent to build a wall—a vital task, but definitely not the final assignment. The purpose of the wall was to contain, to pro-

tect, and to give the people of God an identity. The wall was merely a means to an end.

Discerning leaders know the difference. They avoid tunnel vision, choosing to view the whole scene, not just their own contributions. They observe how the whole project fits into the grander scheme. Nehemiah made provisions for the final completion of God's full plan. He wisely avoided turning the wall into a monument to himself, or to the people involved. He entertained no inflated opinions of the brick-and-mortar project. To him the wall afforded the people a useful and helpful environment (the means) in order to experience a revival that would have eternal ramifications (the end).

If you are careful to observe Nehemiah's leadership in this chapter, you will find a consistent theme: *unselfishness.* Unconcerned about having his name in lights, Nehemiah stepped aside and strengthened the overall project with fresh reinforcements—people such as Ezra, who was better than he in teaching Scripture. And as Ezra did his job, Nehemiah stood among the people applying the truth he heard proclaimed. It posed no problem for him to step aside and have his wall project virtually ignored, because a far more significant activity was taking place among the people.

We have all seen leaders who try to make the project or the job about themselves. Rather than serve the needs of their followers, they turn their position into a means of self-aggrandizement and pride. They are nauseating examples of excessive image building. One authority, speaking of this type of leader, declared rather forcefully:

The leader may consciously enjoy a feeling of superiority and aloofness, showing itself in condescension, vanity, conceit and self-pride. He may demand too much adulation and personal loyalty, and therefore try to surround himself with sycophants, "yes-men" and "rubber stamps." He may want his own way too much and too often, and be too opinionated and obstinate about taking counsel with his colleagues and followers.[2]

From the very start Nehemiah refused all temptations to turn the wall project into an ego trip. He was satisfied to take his place as an Indian—not a chief—among other Indians.

May his tribe increase.

ELEVEN

The Fine Art of Insight

Baseball fans are familiar with the seventh-inning stretch, when everyone gets a chance to stand up and shake out the kinks before you settle down for the final innings. This is precisely what I suggest we do at this point with the Book of Nehemiah. Let's review a few of the previous chapters before we settle down with the last few verses of chapter 8 and proceed with the remainder of Nehemiah's story. To help stretch our mental muscles and sweep away a few cranial cobwebs, I'll approach our brief review from a different perspective.

A GLANCE BACK AND FORTH

Think of the Book of Nehemiah in two main sections. In the first six chapters, we witness the *reconstruction* of a wall; in the last seven, we see the *reinstruction* of the people who built that wall. The first six chapters tell the story of a dominant character (Nehemiah) who was the builder and superintendent over the job and ultimately became governor over the people of Jerusalem. But in the last seven chapters, the leadership shifts to a second major character, Ezra, who was a priest and scribe. Remember, he was the man who sparked the revival by reading and expositing God's Word.

The central theme of the book, threading its way through every episode, is *leadership*—how God uses one person to motivate and encourage others to explore new possibilities, to defy the odds, to overcome inertia and apathy to effect constructive change. In the first six chapters, God uses Nehemiah to teach us sound principles of leadership; in the last seven, He uses Ezra.

In the first part of Nehemiah 8, the revival of the Word of God had a telling effect upon the people. Those who heard the Word read by Ezra were thrilled with what they heard. In fact, verse 8 says that they who read from the book translated it so that they gave the sense of it, and the result was *understanding*. In other words, the people who had built the walls, and were now secure behind those walls, began to receive input from God's Word. And it motivated them.

INPUT VERSUS INSIGHT

For a full day the people of Jerusalem had gathered facts from the Scripture. Let's call it "surface input." They absorbed an understanding of the facts so that their reservoir of biblical knowledge was enlarged. They received *input* but not *insight*. That was to come later.

Then on the second day the heads of fathers' households of all the people, the priests and the Levites were gathered to Ezra the

scribe that they might gain insight into the words of the law.
(Nehemiah 8:13)

The leaders of homes (the fathers) and the religious leaders
(priests and Levites) gathered around Ezra to gain insight from God's
Word. The word *insight* is translated from a Hebrew verb that means
"to be prudent," that is, to be wise, to have foresight, to be shrewd
in the practical management of one's daily affairs. It includes the
qualities of discernment and keen awareness.

Insight is an essential trait for leaders. A leader must be able to
see the big picture, to envision the tomorrows of any undertaking, to
visualize the future consequences of today's decisions, to calculate
risk and develop contingencies. He or she must look farther down
the road than those who follow. No leader can afford to remain
entangled in only the tedious details of today.

Knowledge does not automatically create insight. Vast knowledge of
Bible facts won't make anyone more insightful. I have seen spiritual leaders with advanced academic degrees, having been taught the contents of
the Bible systematically for years, still lacking insight. The corporate,
military, and political worlds are also rife with leaders who, for all their
education, cannot see past the edge of their desks. Tragic, but true.

Remember the twelve disciples who helped Jesus serve the fish and
bread to more than five thousand people? As they watched the loaves
and fish multiply in His hands, you'd think they would have learned
that He could exercise power over any circumstance in life, that nothing was beyond His ability. Yet only a few hours later, they demonstrated that the lesson failed to create insight.

Jesus had them take a boat (without Him) across the Sea of

Galilee. The sky grew dark as the clouds gathered for a squall. As the storm winds blew, the disciples shook with fear. Then Jesus arrived, walking on the waves.

> Then He got into the boat with them, and the wind stopped; and they were utterly astonished, for they had not gained any insight from the incident of the loaves, but their heart was hardened. (Mark 6:51–52)

They had been exposed to His immense power over the elements before, they had seen His miracles and heard His teaching, but their knowledge failed to create discernment. They had received input but not insight.

Leaders may be able to spout theory about a job and have a head full of knowledge concerning proper management, directing people, and accomplishing objectives. But leading with insight is a completely different matter.

For about five years I worked in a machine shop—first as an apprentice and finally as a journeyman machinist. One of my foremen was a man who knew the trade as you know the palm of your hand. Seasoned for more than thirty years, his knowledge of the machinery and machine process could not be matched. Yet he possessed very little insight. He lacked wisdom and foresight when interacting with the men who worked under him. This led to a number of conflicts and heavy turnover of personnel in his department. No man in the shop knew more about the trade or less about leading others than he, and the whole company suffered for his lack.

PURSUING INSIGHT

Nehemiah 8:13–15 reveals three specific factors that help a leader develop the essential quality of insight. First, *it takes time.*

> On the second day the heads of fathers' households of all the people, the priests and the Levites were gathered to Ezra the scribe that they might gain insight into the words of the law. (Nehemiah 8:13)

No one suddenly becomes wise. David declared in Psalm 119:100 that you don't have to be old to have understanding. Nevertheless, there's no such thing as instant insight. A novice cannot expect insight to come quickly. Note that the people of Jerusalem came back to Ezra on the second day. They had processed what they learned and then returned for more.

Second, *it takes the right people.* Note also that in verse 13, the men sought out a specific individual, Ezra, that they might gain insight from him.

I often recall with great delight my days as a pastoral intern between my second and third years at Dallas Theological Seminary. Ray Stedman, pastor of Peninsula Bible Church in Palo Alto, California, had invited my wife, Cynthia, and me to spend the summer of 1961 working at the church. I determined to gain a working knowledge of how a church functions on a practical level. I also had been praying that God would allow me to rub shoulders with some wise and godly men. I didn't know enough to realize it then, but I was a young leader seeking insight.

On several occasions I had the privilege of spending time with Dr. Dick Hillis, the former president of Overseas Crusades. I mined several nuggets of insight from that experience. I also benefited from my lengthy time with Bob Smith, Ray Stedman's close associate for many years. What rich memories I have! I can't recall any "facts" those two men taught me, but the insights I gained still shape my thinking and my leading.

A third factor necessary in the pursuit of insight: *the right attitude.* Verse 13 mentions that the "heads of fathers' households of all the people, the priests and the Levites" were gathered to learn from Ezra. I'm sure some of them were older than the scribe; some were grandfathers, others were priests. These men were members of Ezra's peer group; yet they said, "Teach us." They demonstrated a genuine desire to learn.

Sometimes the Lord wants the insight we need to come through our peers. But if we are to learn from them, we must come with the right attitude.

Many years ago, I spoke at a family conference where I met a young couple with several small children. They looked and sounded like a Christian family, yet I could see that they were absolutely miserable. I was certain divorce was simmering on the back burner of their minds and would eventually boil over. As the week progressed, the couple listened and applied the principles from God's Word.

Another conference speaker, Olan Hendrix, spoke in the mornings on the making of the man of God, and his messages seemed to dovetail beautifully with my comments during the evening sessions on "Insights into Family Living," where I shared things pertaining to husband-wife, parent-child relationships.

As the week unfolded, the father hung on every word. The mother had her Bible open and stayed right with us from passage to passage. On the last day of the conference, the young couple came up to my wife and me and said, "We want you to know that this week has been a one-hundred-eighty-degree turnaround experience for us. When we came, we were ready to separate. We're going back stronger than we have ever been in our marriage." Now that's the sort of thing that makes you want to throw your arms up and say, "Hallelujah!"

Unfortunately, another story of a father is just as heartbreaking as the first is heartwarming. Attending the same conference with the same speakers, hearing the same truths uttered in the same surroundings, and following the same schedule, another father shut down. He attended the first few sessions but, by and by, the guilt mounted and the feeling of conviction grew so deep that he wanted to escape. He debated with himself through the night and, by morning, decided to leave and not come back. His family left hurting—even more than when they first arrived.

The difference between the first couple and this man can be summed up in one word: attitude. A teachable, receptive, humble spirit remains open to learning from anyone at any time.

Some people come to meetings or church services and it does nothing for them. In fact, it turns them off. Others cannot get enough. Like sponges, they soak up every drop of Living Water that drips from the pages of Scripture. As they grow deeper and stronger, I think to myself, "Man, there's no end to this. This is the most exciting thing I have ever seen!" But the person with an unteachable attitude, a closed heart, will never gain insight until he or she decides to exchange pride for a teachable spirit.

Let's review before proceeding. To gain insight, leaders need time: *time* to think, to meditate, to soak up the whole scene. Next, leaders need to learn from the *right people*. Insight is often "rubbed off" from one life to another. Finally, insight comes as we choose the right *attitude*—an open, teachable mind. These three qualities alone will help make you a unique leader.

The Results of Insight

When we get beneath surface facts and start to traffic in the realm of in-depth truth, two things usually happen: we walk in greater obedience, and we discover genuine happiness. The leaders in Nehemiah's day experienced both.

> They found written in the law how the Lord had commanded through Moses that the sons of Israel should live in booths during the feast of the seventh month. So they proclaimed and circulated a proclamation in all their cities and in Jerusalem, saying, "Go out to the hills, and bring olive branches and wild olive branches, myrtle branches, palm branches and branches of other leafy trees, to make booths, as it is written." (Nehemiah 8:14–15)

As I imagine the scene, I cannot suppress a smile. God told them to go live in booths. Intelligent, grown men—all respected leaders—were to go out, fetch some branches and sticks, and make crude, temporary shelters for their families to live in. Imagine that! But out of obedience, they built and lived in those homemade shacks as God had required.

Can't you see Sanballat and Tobiah standing outside the wall? The citizens of Jerusalem were entering and leaving through the newly built gates, looking for sticks and branches.

The enemies ask, "Where are you going?"

"I've got to go get some sticks."

"You're going to go get some what?"

"We're going to go get some sticks."

"For what?"

"For shacks."

"You're going to go get some sticks to build shacks?"

"Right. Come on, kids. There are some branches over here. I need you to carry a handful back."

After a while, they have enough sticks and branches to construct their crude little shelters. Old Sanballat is still looking over the wall, taking it all in. Some guy up on his roof assembles a little lean-to, and it's no beauty! These shacks were rugged to say the least, and they were all over the city of Jerusalem. Sanballat must have shaken his head in amazement and mumbled, "What a strange group of people; and look at those miserable shacks." Nevertheless, as strange as it appeared, the people obeyed.

When God gives you insight (not just knowledge), you say, "Lord, take over. Nothing in my life is private and I'm not proud. Here are the keys." Total, unreserved obedience comes as a result of gaining insight.

Now take note of Nehemiah 8:17:

The entire assembly of those who had returned from the captivity made booths and lived in them. The sons of Israel had indeed not done so from the days of Joshua the son of Nun to that day . . . (Nehemiah 8:17)

They obeyed. Those men said, "God says build a booth; so we'll build a booth."

And amazing though it may sound, those people were happier than they had ever been. "And there was great rejoicing," wrote Nehemiah. I can't explain how it happens, but when you do what is right, regardless of your economic status, you're happy. When you do what is wrong, you may make millions, but you're miserable.

But how could a family live happily in a little shack? They were happy because they were obedient. Because the fathers in the home had gained insight as leaders, they had obeyed the Lord completely. And God gave them contentment, which led to happiness.

Let's face it, your average, standard bosses are a dime a dozen. People in authority over others are found in abundance. In every sizable corporation, organization, or military unit, there are those who give orders and outrank the majority. But few of them are leaders with insight, that is, perspective, wisdom, or a depth of awareness. With that single quality at work in your leadership, you'll be a rare find!

Believe me, insightful leadership is attainable. Nehemiah had it. So did Ezra. But they had no "corner" on the virtue. No one does. It is available to all who are willing to pay the price. Insight not only gives you good perspective on the past and the ability to face the future with confidence and vision, it will also give you an honest appraisal of *yourself*, especially in the area of priorities.

In fact, priorities are what my next chapter is all about.

TWELVE

Four-Dimensional Praying

Of all the disciplines a leader must maintain, nothing—let me repeat, *nothing*—is more vital to success than prayer. Leaders can—and often do—lead without prayer, but after fifty-five years in various leadership roles in industry, the military, and the ministry, I am more than ever convinced of the importance of prayer. Leaders who don't make prayer a priority don't know what they are missing. Whatever is accomplished would be far greater if he or she approached each decision, each challenge, each critical juncture from a kneeling position.

I realize that my role as a pastor shapes my perspective. But if you are a leader in the secular arena, don't flip to the next chapter too quickly. This essential element of leadership applies to you just as much (if not more) than someone in vocational Christian ministry. Your leadership role may play out in the secular arena, but you are a spiritual creature. You may not be able to make prayer a public part of your leading (although you may be surprised), but prayer and the principles illustrated by Nehemiah's example will make you a more effective leader. Furthermore, it could transform your organization in positive ways you never before imagined.

As we approach the topic of prayer, let's begin with an assessment. Carefully consider the following five questions . . . but before you do, make a commitment. Commit to telling yourself the honest truth, no matter how uncomfortable it feels. Unless you reveal them, no one will ever know your answers except the Lord.

First, *are you satisfied with your prayer life?*

Second, *do you pray with confidence?*

Third, *when someone says to you, "Please pray about this," do you?* After three days have passed, are you able to recall the prayer request well enough to follow up with the friend or family member?

Fourth, *if you were asked to name four or five specific matters you have taken to the Lord in prayer this past week, could you do so without hesitation?*

Fifth, *is your time in the Word of God balanced with time in meaningful prayer?*

Now, let's grade your quiz.

If you answered *yes* to all five questions, you may ignore this chapter and turn to the next one with my complete blessing. In fact, I would greatly appreciate your praying for me!

If you answered *yes* to three or four, I commend you, but I'd say that you have some room for improvement. However, the people you lead should be grateful that the Lord is in charge of the organization.

If you had to respond with *no* four or five times, I have good news! Your journey to becoming a more effective leader is about to take a giant leap forward. The discipline of prayer will do more to equip you than any leadership manual or seminar, more than any new insight or impressive strategy.

The Superstitions of Prayer

Before we look at the four dimensions of prayer, let me clear up several common misconceptions. First, prayer is not our attempt to gain the Lord's favor or to get Him to help us achieve our goals. Søren Kierkegaard, a philosopher whose theology left much to be desired, nevertheless understood the nature of prayer better than many. He wrote, "The prayer does not change God, but it changes the one who offers it."[1] Rather than changing God's mind to agree with ours, the goal of prayer is to align our thinking to His so that our plans glorify Him and our decisions accomplish the highest and best good for all concerned—most especially our followers and our organization.

Second, prayer is not the means by which we tap into a limitless reservoir of power to ensure success. This belief has more in common with the New Age movement than with Christianity. The Lord is not an impersonal source of power waiting to propel the desires of men and women—even those having the best intentions to do good. God is a very real personality. He is autonomous, He has a will, and He makes choices. He helps some while hindering others, all according to His plan, motivated by His grace, and completely independent of anyone's merit.

Third, there is no magic formula to prayer. This is perhaps the most common misconception because it appeals to our old sinful nature. I will confess that sometimes I want something so badly that I am tempted to commit the same error as one of the great theologians, Linus Van Pelt.

Offering a prayer according to a certain formula or ritual in the hope that it will somehow get us what we want—even when what we want is entirely righteous and good—is no different than a witch doctor's pagan incantation. It's just as superstitious and it's grievous to the Lord. He created us for the purpose of relationship and has invited us to commune with Him on a personal level. Therefore, when we approach Him as we would a vending machine, we debase a very great privilege.

The Lord already wants to provide what's best for us and those we lead, so we don't need to do anything to persuade or convince Him. However, that's not to say that how we approach the discipline of prayer is irrelevant. Nehemiah's example illustrates several principles that every leader would do well to study and implement.

The Example of a Praying Leader

Nehemiah 9:5–38 is the longest record of a prayer in all of Scripture. When the Bible records a significant prayer, it usually captures the essence of what the person said. According to Nehemiah 9:3, this prayer consumed a fourth of a twelve-hour Jewish day. What we have recorded in the Bible is a condensed version of what was originally a three-hour prayer.

Far more important than the time spent in prayer is the attitude of the people. They approached the Lord with genuine humility and purity of heart:

> Now on the twenty-fourth day of this month the sons of Israel assembled with fasting, in sackcloth and with dirt upon them. (Nehemiah 9:1)

Someone in our modern Western culture might ask, "Why in the world did they go without food, dress in burlap, and pour ashes on their heads?" In some extreme instances, troubled people in the Bible tore their clothes and even sat on a heap of ashes for days at a time.

Many have mistaken these actions to be ways in which people gained God's attention or sympathy. Some even suppose them to be good deeds the Lord will reward by granting the suffering that they desire. However, all of these actions were either outward expressions of inner realities, or serve to prepare the heart of the person to commune with the Lord.

Throughout Scripture, people fasted in order to set aside the interruptions of life so they might give complete, undivided attention to the Lord. During the established time, they didn't have to bother with meal preparation or cleanup. Furthermore, the hunger pangs prompted them to pray.

Sackcloth was heavy, coarse material, typically made from black goat's hair and often used to make bags. It was a terribly uncomfortable garment, so it was an appropriate outward symbol of inner anguish, which could be grief due to tragedy or humiliation because of sin. For the Jews in the Book of Nehemiah, the sackcloth expressed their repentance of past sin.

Every town had a place where garbage and dung were taken to be burned and where ashes continually accumulated. So ancient societies naturally associated ashes with detestable things, even death. Pouring dust or ashes over one's head expressed the inner anguish of someone at the lowest depths of sorrow, saying, in effect, "I have been brought so low, I am like rubbish to be burned."

When Job lost his wealth, his health, and all ten of his children, he tore his garments, poured ashes on his head, and sat on the town ash heap (Job 2:8). And when his counselor-friends came to bring him comfort, they did the same, identifying themselves with Job's sorrow (Job 2:12–13). When the king of Nineveh heard from Jonah that the Lord was going to destroy the great city, he repented in sackcloth and ashes (Jonah 3:6). When Israel experienced defeat at Ai under the leadership of Joshua, the great leader responded by tearing his robes and pouring dust on his head before the Ark of the Covenant (Joshua 7:6).

So, in Nehemiah's day, when the Jews gathered at the wall for prayer, they came in sackcloth and covered with ashes, not to impress God with their piety or to gain His sympathy. Their coarse, black garments and ashen heads reflected the condition of their hearts.

They came before the Lord with genuinely humble spirits, heartsick over their sin.

PRAYER IN FOUR DIRECTIONS

Having gathered for the purpose of prayer as a community, they began with three solid hours of worship. The priests then called the people to prayer. That time in prayer can be divided into four distinct movements.

Looking Up (Nehemiah 9:5–6)

> O may Your glorious name be blessed
> And exalted above all blessing and praise!
> You alone are the Lord.
> You have made the heavens,
> The heaven of heavens with all their host,
> The earth and all that is on it,
> The seas and all that is in them.
> You give life to all of them
> And the heavenly host bows down before You.
> (Nehemiah 9:5–6)

The Jews opened their prayer as all prayer should begin, with praise. I so often hear prayers that begin with a short, obligatory thanks before moving quickly to the wish list. It is rare to hear genuine praise, which is simply the practice of putting all thoughts of self aside to concentrate on adoration of God, and God alone—for His character, for His attributes, for His unmatched qualities.

Their prayer begins with an awe-inspired look straight up into the mysteries and magnificence of God's wondrous person. They praise His name, His exalted position as sovereign ruler of the universe and all that lives in it. Furthermore, they recognize His utter uniqueness and unparalleled character.

By the way, I'm convinced that the more you dwell on the sovereignty and goodness of God, recognizing that *nothing* happens outside His consent, that no event—good or bad—comes to you that hasn't first passed through His fingers, the greater peace you will experience. Accepting His sovereignty and surrendering to His ways are probably the most difficult, yet most productive choices that a person can make. And that begins by recognizing and adoring God as King and ultimate Ruler of life.

Nevertheless, we must never think that we are doing Him any favors by giving Him praise. This is not about stroking God's ego. He invites our worship, but he needs nothing from us. One of my favorite writers, A. W. Tozer, put it this way:

Since He is the Being supreme over all, it follows that God cannot be elevated. Nothing is above Him, nothing beyond Him. Any motion in His direction is elevation for the creature; away from Him, descent. He holds His position out of Himself and by leave of none. As no one can promote Him, so no one can degrade Him. It is written that He upholds all things by the word of His power. How can He be raised or supported by the things He upholds?

Were all human beings suddenly to become blind, still the sun would shine by day and the stars by night, for these things owe nothing to the millions who benefit from their light. So, were every man on earth to become atheist, it could not affect God in any way. He is what He is in Himself without regard to any other. To believe in Him adds nothing to His perfections; to doubt Him takes nothing away. . . .

Probably the hardest thought of all for our natural egotism to entertain is that God does not need our help.[2]

While praise is often the last thing we think about during prayer, it will be the only thing on our minds in heaven.

Looking Back (Nehemiah 9:7–31)

The next section of the prayer is a careful review of Israel's history with a particular focus on God's faithfulness. It starts with the very beginning of Jewish history, the call of Abraham to enter a covenant with God:

> You are the Lord God, who chose Abram and brought him out from Ur of the Chaldees, and gave him the name Abraham. You found his heart faithful before You, and made a covenant with him to give him the land of the Canaanite, of the Hittite and the Amorite, of the Perizzite, the Jebusite and the Girgashite—to give it to his descendants. And You have fulfilled Your promise, for You are righteous. (Nehemiah 9:7–8)

This is, essentially, the story of Genesis. The Lord made an unconditional covenant with Abraham and worked diligently to fulfill His promises despite the failures of Abraham and his descendants.

Then the Jews recalled the miraculous working of God to bring them out of slavery in Egypt, through the Red Sea to freedom:

> You saw the affliction of our fathers in Egypt, and heard their cry by the Red Sea. Then You performed signs and wonders against Pharaoh, against all his servants and all the people of his land; for You knew that they acted arrogantly toward them, and made a name for Yourself as it is this day. You divided the sea before them, so they passed through the midst of the sea on dry ground; and their pursuers You hurled into the depths, like a stone into raging waters. And with a pillar of cloud You led them by day, and with a pillar of fire by night to light for them the way in which they were to go. (Nehemiah 9:9–12)

Whenever the people of God began to doubt His promises, or worry that He might have given up on them, or become discouraged in the midst of a trial, they typically rehearsed the Exodus story. This reminded them of the foolish question their ancestors once asked—while pressed against the Red Sea with Pharaoh's army bearing down fast—"Did you lead us into the desert to die?!" (Exodus 14:11–12) The answer they received at the Red Sea resounded down the corridors of history and echoed off each obstacle: "Of course not!" This is the story of Exodus.

Their prayer then recounted the Lord's giving of the Law through Moses and His preservation of the Hebrew people in the wilderness:

> Then You came down on Mount Sinai, and spoke with them from heaven; You gave them just ordinances and true laws, good

statutes and commandments. So You made known to them Your holy sabbath, and laid down for them commandments, statutes and law, through Your servant Moses. You provided bread from heaven for them for their hunger, You brought forth water from a rock for them for their thirst, and You told them to enter in order to possess the land which You swore to give them. (Nehemiah 9:13–15)

The Lord entrusted His Word on earth to Israel, whom He wanted to settle on prime real estate for the purpose of reaching the world. This is the story of Leviticus. The people would obey; He would prosper them; the world would ask, "Why are the Hebrew so content?"; they would answer, "Worship our God and share our contentment." But . . .

From Sinai to Kadesh-Barnea and back into the wilderness for forty years of chastisement, they frustrated God's plan by repeatedly turning away. The Jews in Nehemiah's day refused to ignore their forefathers' disobedience.

But they, our fathers, acted arrogantly; they became stubborn and would not listen to Your commandments. They refused to listen, and did not remember Your wondrous deeds which You had performed among them; so they became stubborn and appointed a leader to return to their slavery in Egypt. But You are a God of forgiveness, gracious and compassionate, slow to anger and abounding in lovingkindness; and You did not forsake them. Even when they made for themselves a calf of molten metal and said, "This is your God who brought you up from

Egypt," and committed great blasphemies, You, in Your great
compassion, did not forsake them in the wilderness; the pillar of
cloud did not leave them by day, to guide them on their way, nor
the pillar of fire by night, to light for them the way in which they
were to go. You gave Your good Spirit to instruct them, Your
manna You did not withhold from their mouth, and You gave
them water for their thirst. Indeed, forty years You provided for
them in the wilderness and they were not in want; their clothes
did not wear out, nor did their feet swell. (Nehemiah 9:16–21)

This is the story of Numbers and Deuteronomy.

Despite their recurring fits of doubt, grumbling, rebellion, and
outright idolatry, the Lord brought them into the Promised Land,
settled them, and began to prosper them:

You also gave them kingdoms and peoples, and allotted them to
them as a boundary. They took possession of the land of Sihon the
king of Heshbon and the land of Og the king of Bashan. You
made their sons numerous as the stars of heaven, and You brought
them into the land which You had told their fathers to enter and
possess. So their sons entered and possessed the land. And You
subdued before them the inhabitants of the land, the Canaanites,
and You gave them into their hand, with their kings and the peoples of the land, to do with them as they desired. They captured
fortified cities and a fertile land. They took possession of houses
full of every good thing, hewn cisterns, vineyards, olive groves,
fruit trees in abundance. So they ate, were filled and grew fat, and
reveled in Your great goodness. (Nehemiah 9:22–25)

This is the story of Joshua.

> But they became disobedient and rebelled against You, and cast Your law behind their backs and killed Your prophets who had admonished them so that they might return to You, and they committed great blasphemies. Therefore You delivered them into the hand of their oppressors who oppressed them, but when they cried to You in the time of their distress, You heard from heaven, and according to Your great compassion You gave them deliverers who delivered them from the hand of their oppressors. But as soon as they had rest, they did evil again before You; therefore You abandoned them to the hand of their enemies, so that they ruled over them. When they cried again to You, You heard from heaven, and many times You rescued them according to Your compassion, and admonished them in order to turn them back to Your law. Yet they acted arrogantly and did not listen to Your commandments but sinned against Your ordinances, by which if a man observes them he shall live. And they turned a stubborn shoulder and stiffened their neck, and would not listen. (Nehemiah 9:26–29)

This is the story of Judges. Seven bewildering cycles of prosperity, sin, decline, oppression, repentance, and deliverance, then back around to prosperity again, though less than before. It's a tragic, sickening, downward spiral into national chaos on every level—spiritual, political, economic, and social.

Nevertheless, the Lord remained faithful. Upon the coronation of David, Israel entered its golden era, a brilliant time of national faithfulness, expansion, and prosperity. The country finally seemed to have pulled itself together under the leadership of "a man after God's own heart" (1 Samuel 13:14). But behind closed doors, the king compromised in private. His son, Solomon, compromised in broad daylight. And subsequent kings plunged Israel back into the dark ages of idolatry.

> However, You bore with them for many years, and admonished them by Your Spirit through Your prophets, yet they would not give ear. Therefore You gave them into the hand of the peoples of the lands. Nevertheless, in Your great compassion You did not make an end of them or forsake them, for You are a gracious and compassionate God. (Nehemiah 9:30–31)

This is the story of the kings, and the captivity of Israel under Babylon and Persia.

As we have seen, a substantial portion of this prayer took an intensive look back into Jewish history to highlight a consistent theme: God's faithfulness despite human failure. A realistic view of the past can provide the very best perspective on the present and can suggest ways to ensure a better future. It's a difficult exercise, but I can assure you it holds astounding potential for the leader who is willing to put forth the effort.

One evening, back when our children were still living at home, I announced at the dinner table, "Tonight, we're going to take some time for reflection." For the next hour, the Swindolls looked back on our history. Cynthia and I recalled the first years of our marriage, from 1955 to 1959, when we began to give God complete control of our life together. We told of the time we prepared for ministry from

1959 to 1963, during which time we brought our first child into the world.

We paused as one of our girls offered a prayer of thanksgiving for the birth of her older brother. Cynthia thanked God for the things we learned during seminary and I thanked Him for the church into which we invested our lives.

And so, we reviewed each segment of our family history, pausing at the major transitions, including each child's birth, so that we could offer a prayer of praise and thanks for the Lord's provision and sovereign direction. What a marvelous time! We experienced a greater bond with each other and, more importantly, with the Lord as a family.

What a valuable activity for a family, a church, or any organization!

Looking In (Nehemiah 9:32–37)

With their checkered past and the Lord's faithfulness fresh on their minds, the Jews took stock of their present situation:

> Now therefore, our God, the great, the mighty, and the awesome God, who keeps covenant and lovingkindness, do not let all the hardship seem insignificant before You, which has come upon us, our kings, our princes, our priests, our prophets, our fathers and on all Your people, from the days of the kings of Assyria to this day. However, You are just in all that has come upon us; for You have dealt faithfully, but we have acted wickedly. For our kings, our leaders, our priests and our fathers have not kept Your law or paid attention to Your commandments and Your admonitions with which You have admonished them. But they, in their own

kingdom, with Your great goodness which You gave them, with the broad and rich land which You set before them, did not serve You or turn from their evil deeds. Behold, we are slaves today, and as to the land which You gave to our fathers to eat of its fruit and its bounty, behold, we are slaves in it. Its abundant produce is for the kings whom You have set over us because of our sins; they also rule over our bodies and over our cattle as they please, so we are in great distress. (Nehemiah 9:32–37)

In this honest look at the present, I find only one petition: "Do not let all the hardship seem insignificant before You."

I find this element of the prayer particularly authentic in its pain and humility. When the suffering we endure as a consequence of our own sin bears down, it's natural to wonder how much the Lord cares about our pain. If it's a result of our own sin, we deserve to hurt, don't we? So why *should* He care? Like most of us in our weaker moments, the Jews projected their own fleshly attitudes onto God. How easy to forget God's mercy, God's grace.

Let me encourage you to pray honestly and express how you feel, (even if it isn't theologically astute) at that moment of anguish. Dare to pray what you authentically think and feel. If you're doubtful of His love for you, tell Him! If you're angry with Him, express it. Confess it. He already knows everything about you. He won't be shocked. You aren't hiding anything from Him.

I'm not suggesting you curse God or treat Him irreverently. However, don't withhold yourself from Him. Bring all of you, including your bad attitude, your confused theology, your irrational emotions, your bewildered, heartrending cry for compassion. He's loved you in spite of your sin; He certainly won't reject you for praying imperfectly.

In verse 36, the repentant nation of Israel acknowledged, "As to the land which You gave to our fathers to eat of its fruit and its bounty, behold, we are slaves in it." They acknowledged the irony of their current situation and accepted complete responsibility for their status as servants to a godless, pagan regime.

No leader can effectively chart a new path toward healing and recovery without first acknowledging his or her organization's present reality. If earnings are negative and plummeting, the CEO must accept the hard, cold truth without the distortion of optimistic or pessimistic lenses. If the church is wracked with division, the pastor must peel away all the masking to expose the cracks. If the company is rife with incompetence, the leader must recognize the need for replacement or training before setting substantive goals. Quite often, the very act of stating present realities will suggest the appropriate solutions. God loves it when we're vulnerable and painfully honest before Him.

Looking Ahead (Nehemiah 9:38)

The fourth and final direction of prayer, having looked upward, backward, and inward, is forward—ahead, eyes front. What follows is a simple statement of intent on the part of the Jews, a course of action they immediately pursued.

> Now because of all this we are making an agreement in writing; and on the sealed document are the names of our leaders, our Levites and our priests. (Nehemiah 9:38)

The specific plan they devised and documented is the subject of the next chapter. A quick scan of Nehemiah 10 reveals that the new direction was very different than the old. Their history could be summarized in a single word: disobedience. Their commitment, as expressed in their official letter of intent to the Lord, was obedience. They committed to answer every significant failure in Genesis through 2 Chronicles with a specific remedy. Furthermore, they recorded their commitments, read them in public, and then signed the document in the presence of God and witnesses.

Now *that's* what I call an action plan!

A Challenge to Strong Leaders

I want to issue a challenge. My challenge is only to those leaders who genuinely want to achieve success—whatever your arena and wherever you lead. I'm not restricting this to ministry or to the spiritual realm in secular contexts. Define "success" however you want to. If record fourth-quarter earnings is what defines success in the eyes of your organization, then this is for you as well.

I challenge you to set aside an afternoon, find a place where you can be alone, and compose a prayer using Nehemiah's model. Write it out, taking each of the four dimensions in order. Think about your organization and compose a prayer that looks up, looks back, and looks in. Then allow the experience to suggest how to move the organization forward as you look ahead. If nothing specific comes to mind, make that your petition: "Lord, help me discover the best path forward."

If, on the other hand, the plan seems clear, document it in the form of a prayer. If you have a detailed business plan, write it out as a prayer, committing the strategies to the glory of God and yourself to implementing them.

Once you have composed the prayer (which may become lengthy), commit to praying at least a portion of the plan each day. I recommend spending a few minutes on it, three or four times throughout the day, and a significant amount of time either early in the morning or at night before retiring. Consider recruiting others to join you in reviewing and revising the prayer, and then praying through it as a team.

I guarantee something wonderful will happen. Something will change for the better. It might be the organization, it could be the plan or the surrounding circumstances, or it might even be *you*. Regardless, the Lord wants to be a significant part of your leadership and the success of your organization. I challenge you to invite Him into the process through the discipline of prayer. As Richard Chenevix Trench wrote, "We must not conceive of prayer as overcoming God's reluctance, but as laying hold of His highest willingness."[3]

I challenge you: *Lay Hold!*

Thirteen

Putting First Things First

A California industrialist was addressing a group of executives at a leadership seminar. His topic concerned employee motivation—how to get the job done while encouraging the enthusiasm and commitment of others. He offered a lot of helpful advice, but one concept in particular has stuck in my head: "There are two things that are the most difficult to get people to do: to think . . . and to do things in the order of their importance."

That concept touches a nerve in every leader. How difficult it is to find a person who thinks first—and then acts! Most of us usually do the opposite. Equally difficult is helping people maintain proper priorities and to use time wisely. Not only does the leader wrestle with ways to help others think and put first things first, he struggles to do this himself. And the degree to which the leader can maintain these two disciplines will determine how well he or she can lead.

I admire Nehemiah because he was a man who thought before he acted and kept his priorities clearly in view.

TAKING TIME TO THINK

As you recall, Nehemiah didn't bring a group of people into Jerusalem and immediately have them start to stack up bricks and stones, mix mortar, and erect a wall. He spent four months in uninterrupted thought before doing anything. He thought through the vision before he ever shared it with anyone else. He pored over it in concentrated thought before God. Only then did he explain his objective and begin to build a wall.

When opposition came, he didn't instantly retaliate; he thought it over. He prayerfully planned the best way to handle the interruption or the opposition, and then he acted wisely. When the time came to develop the plan for a righteous lifestyle, what we would call a good government, he didn't suddenly plunge into it; he first spent some more time *thinking*. And the people, apparently imitating the thoughtful approach exemplified by Nehemiah, also went to God in prayer. Their prayer, the longest recorded prayer in the Bible (Nehemiah 9:5–38), revealed their utter repentance and confidence in Jehovah. Over a lengthy period of thinking, planning, and reflecting, they came to a conclusion, which is recorded in the last verse of that long prayer. Before we look at that conclusion, let's think about thinking.

Thinking is hard work. Don't kid yourself—coming up with a good plan is usually far more difficult than carrying it out. Leaders who don't plan carefully and who shoot from the hip miss the target—wounding others in the process!

Call me old-fashioned, but I still believe that the husband should be one who steps forward to lead the family. After all, the Bible makes this very clear! Unfortunately, many men are poorly suited to the role of leader, which makes the home a very difficult place for many wives and children.

Wives want to have husbands who think through their philosophy on the home and the family. Few things are more frustrating than trying to serve alongside a man who doesn't know where he's going. Here are some questions the leader of the home should think through:

- What are the goals of the home?

- What is the best way to live and teach Christian convictions?

- Where should we live and why?

- How should the family try to reach neighbors and friends for Christ?

- Why do we want to have children?

- What can we do to help each child become confident and fulfilled?

- Which methods of discipline shall we use?

- What guidelines on teenage dating will we follow?

- What do we want to accomplish on our vacations?

- How involved should we be in the church? In civic affairs? In athletics?

- What are our convictions regarding the entertainment media, such as music, television, movies, and video games?

- How shall we cultivate a close relationship as husband and wife?

Men, that type of thinking is hard work! But what a difference it would make in your leadership in your home if you would think through such issues.

Another set of questions could be drawn up for leaders in the workplace. Leadership begins with a clear objective and a distinct set of values established *in the mind of the leader.*

Thinking includes praying and quietness. We've seen Nehemiah often on his knees. He prayed through vital issues. So must we. We've also seen him quiet, silently thinking through his plans. How very important that was. Free from rush and panic, Nehemiah's deliberate plans gave others a definite sense of confidence. Frequent last-minute changes and impulsive, rash decisions create chaos and diminish the enthusiasm of those who follow, causing them to fear the consequences that could affect them.

Thinking calls for projecting. By backing off and thinking through a plan, the leader is able to travel down his or her projected path intelligently and also consider future inevitabilities—while it is still safe. He or she can anticipate risks and develop contingency plans in advance. Jesus spoke of the wisdom of thinking ahead and planning this way:

> For which one of you, when he wants to build a tower, does not first sit down and calculate the cost to see if he has enough to complete it? Otherwise, when he has laid a foundation and is not able to finish, all who observe it begin to ridicule him, saying, "This man began to build and was not able to finish." Or what king, when he sets out to meet another king in battle, will not first sit down and consider whether he is strong enough with ten thousand men to encounter the one coming against him with twenty thousand? (Luke 14:28–31)

Leaders who expect to be respected and followed must, first and foremost, be *thinkers*.

DOCUMENTING THE PRIORITIES

As we consider the story of Nehemiah, we find the people anxious to alter their lives. In short, they determined to do things in the order of their importance. First things were to come first. The people were thoughtfully remembering the past and saying to the Lord, "Because of all these things we have brought before You, our Father, we want to establish some priorities. We are making an agreement in writing." Nehemiah 9 deals with these priorities. In this lengthy chapter, the people pour out their souls to God. They formally declare their dependence. In effect, they develop a new set of priorities, which they declare in writing.

The Document

> Now because of all this we are making an agreement in writing;
> and on the sealed document are the names of our leaders, our
> Levites and our priests. (Nehemiah 9:38)

This is the action of a people who are serious about putting first things first. And signatures accompanied this "sealed document" (see Nehemiah 10:1–27) so that all would know they meant business. You see, establishing clear priorities is extremely important. Unfortunately, many who read this will nod in agreement—but will not follow through. The people of Jerusalem followed through on their intentions by establishing a charter. And they sealed it with a prayer that said, in effect, "Lord, we don't want our words to be empty. We want our intentions to be a solemn promise, bound by an oath. And we'll sign our names to prove that we'll keep our promise!"

Before we proceed to the promises they made in their document, let's discover something about those who signed the agreement. Nehemiah lists eighty-four names, with Nehemiah's name first. After Nehemiah come the names of twenty-two priests (see Nehemiah 10:1–8); seventeen Levites (see Nehemiah 10:9–18); and forty-four others who were called leaders or heads of homes (see Nehemiah 10:10–27). These were the political, religious, and economic leaders of the community. Each name represented a host of other men, women, and children in Jerusalem who staked their futures with the Lord.

But more important than mere names, is what Nehemiah 10:28–30 says was true of every person that assented to the document, either by signing or by oath:

> Now the rest of the people, the priests, the Levites, the gatekeepers, the singers, the temple servants and all those who had separated themselves from the peoples of the lands to the law of God, their wives, their sons and their daughters, all those who had knowledge and understanding, are joining with their kinsmen, their nobles, and are taking on themselves a curse and an oath to walk in God's law, which was given through Moses, God's servant, and to keep and to observe all the commandments of God our Lord, and His ordinances and His statutes; and that we will not give our daughters to the peoples of the land or take their daughters for our sons. (Nehemiah 10:28–30)

Take note of two facts that identified these people as extraordinary: they had separated themselves from the godless people living around them as well as their pagan lifestyles, and they were wise, discerning people who knew what they were doing. By endorsing the document, a person understood that he and his family were part of God's unique, set-apart people and agreed to live accordingly, rejecting the lifestyles of the pagans living near their community.

They made a decision to put first things first, *regardless* of the situation.

This action, this document, was a crucial choice in the life of Israel. They drove a literary stake into the ground that day, which became their rallying point. They erected a written monument much like the founding documents that made the United States a nation. They drafted and ratified their declaration of dependence and distinction—their constitution. It established their purpose and values, saying, as it were: "We don't care if anyone else in the world lives by this. We will live by it. It will be our guide. Our homes will be distinct. Our philosophy of life will not be like that of those who live outside the walls—or even of some who live within the city's walls. This is something, Lord, that we want to carry out before You."

I want to point out that promises are fine but, as fallen creatures who are given to weakness and second-guessing, so it helps if we *document* our priorities.

As a pastor, I have married countless couples in my forty-plus years of ministry. That translates into a lot of new homes that were established on a promise. It would have been easy for me to just stand in front of them, utter a few religious clichés, wave my hand, pronounce them husband and wife, and walk away whistling "Here Comes the Bride." But I determined never to do that.

As has been my habit and always will be, I require at least three premarital counseling sessions with a couple before agreeing to marry them. Among other things, I ask them to begin formulating their priorities as a couple. I ask them to write them down, to *document* their priorities, which occasionally I read during their ceremony and often weave into the wording of their vows. I then ask them to listen to a tape recording of their ceremony every year when their anniversary rolls around. Hopefully, this annual exercise will reinforce some specifics that will help each couple confirm that they are still on target and what corrections to make if they have veered off course.

I would recommend a similar procedure for someone committing to a college education, or establishing a business, or taking on a large project. Set priorities. Take the time to articulate your purpose, objectives, and values. Put them in writing and share them with someone who can hold you accountable. And when you begin to wander from your chosen path, or when discouragement sets in, he or she can present that document and help you see the importance of staying on course and finishing strong.

The Promises

In Nehemiah 10:29 there is a general promise to *obey* what God had declared. In verse 30, the people specifically said that they would obey Him in their *homes.* They were surrounded by idolatrous, pagan people who marched to a different drumbeat. They could have easily lost their distinctiveness as "the people of God" in that environment, and so the leaders of each home promised, "We will not give our daughters to the peoples of the land or take their daughters for our sons" (Nehemiah 10:30).

They took intermingling with idol-worshipers very seriously. They didn't withdraw or refuse to interact. Yet they didn't shrug their shoulders, yawn, and say, "Kids will be kids," when their children chose friends from among people having no relationship with the Lord.

Distinctive, respectable leaders have unique homes.

The point I want to make very clear is this: When morals of a nation are under stress, the home is the first to suffer. Evangelist Billy Graham put it this way:

> The immutable law of sowing and reaping has held sway. We are now the hapless possessors of moral depravity, and we seek in vain for a cure. The tares of indulgence have overgrown the wheat of moral restraint. Our homes have suffered. . . . When the morals of society are upset, the family is the first to suffer. The home is the basic unit of our society, and a nation is only as strong as her homes.[1]

He wrote those words more than forty years ago! The drug culture had just begun to spread among college-age youth and has since become one of our nation's most enduring problems, accounting for untold millions of dollars wasted and countless lives destroyed. The era of "free love," just beginning to emerge when Graham penned the words above, turned sexually transmitted disease into an epidemic. What became a serious nuisance in the 1970s turned deadly in the 1980s. The "immutable law of sowing and reaping" has indeed held sway.

If you're thinking about documenting a list of priorities for living, I suggest you start with the home. It will make a profound difference in your leadership outside the family as well as within.

Next, the signers promised to *conduct business* in an obedient manner.

> As for the peoples of the land who bring wares or any grain on the sabbath day to sell, we will not buy from them on the sabbath or a holy day; and we will forego the crops the seventh year and the exaction of every debt. (Nehemiah 10:31)

This was a significant promise made by people who knew hunger and could not count on another good day for buying and selling. The peoples of another culture would certainly test their mettle on this point. When the sun rose on Saturday (the Jewish Sabbath) and they saw those who wanted to do business coming over the hills toward Jerusalem, they committed to saying, "We are closed for worship and reflection. We'll do business with you tomorrow." And when the seventh year rolled around, they would allow the fields to lay fallow and take their rest from sowing and reaping until the next year. When a brother owed a debt, they agreed to look upon it as God commanded and would release the fellow Jew from his debt.

This was the God-ordained code of business ethics and they agreed to do business on the up-and-up.

A strong leader always does business with integrity. When he puts in a day's work, he puts in a *day's* work. When she is to check in at a certain time, she is punctual. When he is trusted not to take what does not belong to him, he leaves it. When she completes her expense report, she doesn't pad the record.

Keith Miller puts it this way:

It has never ceased to amaze me that we Christians have developed a kind of selective vision which allows us to be deeply and sincerely involved in worship and church activities and yet almost totally pagan in the day in, day out guts of our business lives . . . and never realize it.[2]

In the nuts and bolts of living, God will honor the person who honors Him. Such a decision deserves a place on any leader's priority list.

The Jews had declared they would put first things first in their homes and in their business activities. Next they turned their attention to their *place of worship*. In Nehemiah 10:32–39 the leader references the "house of the Lord" or the "house of God" no less than nine times. It's not difficult to notice the theme:

We also placed ourselves under obligation to contribute yearly . . . for the service of the house of our God . . . Likewise we cast lots for the supply of wood among the priests, the Levites and the people . . . and that they might bring the first fruits of our ground and the first fruits of all the fruit of every tree to the house of the Lord annually . . . We will also bring the first of our dough, our contributions, the fruit of every tree. (Nehemiah 10:32–35, 37)

Putting it all together, verse 39 concludes: "Thus we will not neglect the house of our God."

We have labeled the priority in this passage the *place of worship*. In Nehemiah's day it was the temple. When they came to the house of God, they brought with them all these things because it was the place of God's dwelling. But when Christ our Lord died, the veil was torn in two; it was split from top to bottom. Where does God live now? On earth He lives in every believer. If you are a believer in Jesus Christ, the house of God is *right within you.* Talk about a mind-boggling concept! Talk about removing the old sacred-secular divisions in life. I'm saying that the place of highest priority in these verses is the inner man where Jesus Christ resides, where the Holy Spirit has built His temple. Paul states it clearly:

> Or do you not know that your body is a temple of the Holy Spirit who is in you, whom you have from God, and that you are not your own? For you have been bought with a price: therefore glorify God in your body. (1 Corinthians 6:19–20)

Are you neglecting the temple? In the days of Nehemiah the temple was not a place where people just walked by and said, "Wow! God lives over there. Have you been there lately?" It was the place where they worshiped with great care and a sensitive, devoted spirit. How are you treating God's house?

I have one other question: Is your temple clean? You're not carrying the principles of leadership in a dirty container, are you? Habits that harm your health will hinder your impact and confuse those who look to you for direction.

Priorities are rather convicting, aren't they?

Key Principles to Remember

There are some very simple—but life-changing—principles that I glean from these verses in Nehemiah 10. The first is that *serious thought precedes any significant change.* You never change areas of your life that have not been given serious thought. We need to schedule some quiet times in our lives, times for thinking and reflection.

When you see a person who has changed from what he or she was a year ago and you ask, "Hey, how did that come about?" the answer will rarely come back, "Oh, it just happened. It's amazing; it surprised even me! I didn't plan for it to happen, I just changed." Instead, he or she will tell you, "I'm glad you asked," and then go on to describe what God did—one, two, three, four. Change comes on the heels of specific, honest thinking about our lives.

Second, *written plans confirm right priorities.* Do you really want to maintain the right priorities? Write them down! I suggest you begin to keep a journal. You may have some ideas floating around in your head, but they need to be nailed down. I learned years ago that complex, ethereal thoughts become straightforward, concrete strategies when spoken or put in ink. Your thoughts may be good, but they will remain forever entangled if they haven't been thought through and written down. The ability to put first things first will elude you until your purpose, objectives, and plans are written out.

Third, *where the world is concerned, distinction and conformity pull us in opposite directions.* Do you want to know today whether you have really conformed to this world or not? Ask yourself, "How distinctive am I?" This has nothing to do with religious activity or how much involvement you have at church. Distinction is a measure of how authentic your ethics and your conduct are when compared to New

Testament Christianity. Look at your life, your home, your work, your worship, and then ask yourself, "Am I really distinct? Could a person get to know the real me and see God's message on display?"

The leaders who have meant the most to me in my life are those who are authentic. They are men and women who have thought before they acted, who have put first things first, and who have maintained their distinctiveness as Christian men and women. I thank God every time I notice a particular contribution one of them has made in my life.

Think. Then do the things that need to be done in the order of their importance. People gravitate to leaders who live by that philosophy. Having met and been with such people, I've never been the same.

FOURTEEN

The Willing Unknowns

The bicentennial celebration of our nation was an unforgettable experience. My wife and I were part of a tour back in 1976 that traveled for two weeks along the East Coast, and we were thrilled by our visits to the sites where America's cradle first rocked. Monuments and memorials, buildings and bridges, towns and tombs told of our nation's past and spoke with more eloquence than mere words. All Americans owe a deep debt of gratitude to great statesmen like George Washington, Thomas Jefferson, Benjamin Franklin, and Patrick Henry—well-known men who deserve credit for their capable leadership and determined zeal.

But there is another body of names and faces equally deserving of our praise. They are the lesser lights, the forgotten heroes, the unknowns, the "nobodies" who paved the way for the "somebodies." Without these willing unknowns, no leader can ever carry out his or her calling. But how easy it is to forget them.

This was brought home to me rather forcefully one day when my family and I were driving down the coast of California from San

Francisco to Los Angeles. As we traveled along, enjoying the crashing surf to our right and the distant mountains to our left, we were laughing, singing, and having a great time. It was one of those delightful moments large families enjoy together. It wasn't long, however, before things got quiet. As we went over the crest of a hill, we saw literally thousands of small white crosses standing at attention in perfect rank and file. Our youngest child leaned toward me and asked, "Daddy, what's all that?" Almost without thinking I answered, "Son, that's a military graveyard. That's a place where they have buried the men and women who died in battle. Few people remember them, son, but they are the reason we are free today." His eyes got big as he gazed in silence across that sacred hillside.

The car remained very quiet as I slowed down so we could look closely at row after row of small, white monuments to courage. All those heroes now lay silent. I confess that a big knot formed in my throat as the words of the poet, John McCrae, came to mind. Writing from the viewpoint of fallen heroes speaking to the living:

> In Flanders fields the poppies blow
> Between the crosses, row on row,
> That mark our place; and in the sky
> The larks, still bravely singing, fly
> Scarce heard amid the guns below.
>
> We are the Dead. Short days ago
> We lived, felt dawn, saw sunset glow,
> Loved and were loved, and now we lie
> In Flanders fields.[1]

As we drove on, I thought of how true that really is. The crosses stand in rows. The larks fly overhead. The cars speed on. Every once in a while, I imagine the unknown dead to say, "Don't forget us. We are the reason you are able to drive and live and move freely." There they lie in long, silent rows, the willing unknowns.

Two dangers lurk in the shadows of leadership. One is the *reluctance* on the part of the leader to become virtually unknown, forgotten, and overlooked in the accomplishment of an objective. The second is the *negligence* of strong natural leaders who fail to recognize others who deserve much of the credit. It's the second danger I want to emphasize in this chapter, but before doing so, let's take time to consider the first.

I'm going to ask you to make a commitment to the Lord to be, if necessary, as unknown as possible in your position of influence. This is a genuine test of strong leadership. If you desire fame and recognition, you will most likely fail as a leader and your efforts will go unrewarded for all eternity. That's not a threat: It's a fact. Jesus spoke directly to this point:

> Beware of practicing your righteousness before men to be noticed by them; otherwise you have no reward with your Father who is in heaven. (Matthew 6:1)

And in even stronger words, He declared:

> You know that the rulers of the Gentiles lord it over them, and their great men exercise authority over them. It is not this way among you, but whoever wishes to become great among you shall be your servant, and whoever wishes to be first among you

shall be your slave; just as the Son of Man did not come to be served, but to serve, and to give His life a ransom for many. (Matthew 20:25–28)

It may sound strange to our twenty-first-century ears, but God is ready to bless some capable leaders who genuinely do not care who receives the glory. Such leaders are all too rare, but what a wonderful discovery when we stumble across a few outstanding people who don't want to be superstars and willingly remain genuine servants.

IDENTIFYING THE UNKNOWNS

Now let's consider the other side of the coin: how to give credit to the many unknowns who delight in filling support positions so that the job will be completed. Several people like this appear in the eleventh chapter of Nehemiah's journal, a chapter we could entitle the "Flanders Field" of the Bible. We find here the crosses of unknown, obscure, forgotten people (with unpronounceable names!). But they represent a massive force that makes the Word of God exciting. You cannot appreciate the names and people of Nehemiah 11, however, if you do not know the reason they appear. Nehemiah 7:1–2 provides a little background information:

Now when the wall was rebuilt and I had set up the doors, and the gatekeepers and the singers and the Levites were appointed, then I put Hanani my brother, and Hananiah the commander of the fortress, in charge of Jerusalem, for he was a faithful man and feared God more than many. (Nehemiah 7:1–2)

The names of these two men are unfamiliar, in fact, nothing more is ever said of them. But they took up ranks among the willing unknowns as delegates who carried out the wishes of Nehemiah, the governor.

Then verse 3 says that Nehemiah set a schedule for the city and established a security force:

> Do not let the gates of Jerusalem be opened until the sun is hot, and while they are standing guard, let them shut and bolt the doors. Also appoint guards from the inhabitants of Jerusalem, each at his post, and each in front of his own house. (Nehemiah 7:3)

With the establishment of order and a police presence, Jerusalem began to show signs of normal life. The city had everything except the most important ingredient—people.

> Now the city was large and spacious, but the people in it were few and the houses were not built. (Nehemiah 7:4)

The city had been without a wall for one hundred sixty years. If my calculations are correct, the Jews spent seventy years in captivity and an additional ninety years passed before Nehemiah came on the scene. So for more than one hundred sixty years, Jerusalem was little more than a barren pile of debris. Anyone foolish enough to live there would have been easy prey for robbers, burglars, and thugs. Instead, the Jews who returned from exile built spacious, lavishly furnished homes in the suburbs. Most of the Jews had forsaken an urban life.

Another reason few people chose to live on the ruins of the destroyed city was the enormous amount of work it required—

debris, stones, and stumps were everywhere. Plenty of land lay out-side the walls that required little or no clearing and would better sup-port the cultivation of crops.

In order to attract willing city dwellers, the Jerusalem Chamber of Commerce had to devise a plan. According to Nehemiah 11:1, the leaders of the people lived within the city, probably to receive an annual bonus or other monetary encouragement. But the rest of the people found living in the surrounding hamlets to be more secure, more comfortable, and more lucrative.

Two factors brought people into Jerusalem. First, the leaders cast lots to bring one out of ten into the urban area. This group was brought by force. It was something like the way the U.S. government drafted men into the military during the Vietnam War. When a man's number came up, he went.

The second method of increasing Jerusalem's population is of even greater interest to us. According to Nehemiah 11:2, *another group volunteered:* "And the people blessed all the men who volunteered to live in Jerusalem." Among the nine-tenths who remained outside the wall, some were strangely moved of God to take up urban dwelling. *Volunteered* is a Hebrew word that means "to impel, to incite from within." The word implies the presence of inner generosity and will-ingness. In other words, down deep inside, these volunteers were impelled by God to move. And they did.

Can you imagine it? These people, living in the suburbs, were chosen by God to move from suburbia into the inner city, and they did it willingly and generously. Had they never volunteered, the city would not have prospered, nor could it have withstood the enemy attacks that came in later years.

Devotion of the Nameless

One scholar has done a rather intricate work of calculation and has estimated that a million or more people lived in areas surrounding Jerusalem. A tenth of those people were forced to move, but a large number of them came inside the city because they were impelled from within. They became, to use my title, "the willing unknowns." The Scripture rarely mentions the name of any one of them.

"Willing unknowns" rarely if ever enjoy recognition for their contributions. In the Book of Exodus, chapter 35, we find a group of people who were skilled craftsmen in embroidery, weaving, and other skills. They added the more refined touches to the tabernacle. Exodus 35 also refers to those who willingly gave their money, their talent, and their time for the service of God. The same Hebrew word for *volunteer* in Nehemiah 7 also appears in Exodus 35. They volunteered themselves to God. Except Moses, the leader, and Aaron, his illustrious brother, hardly another name is recorded for posterity. But the whole tabernacle beautification project would have failed without all those willing unknowns.

Deeds of the Nameless

In Nehemiah 11, I find five specific groups who willingly gave something—even though their giving remained anonymous. We've just read about the first group: "The people blessed all the men who volunteered to live in Jerusalem."

The first group included *those who willingly moved into the city.* They pulled up their domestic roots, left their comfortable homes, started over from scratch, submitted themselves to a government they hadn't elected, and lived in a city policed by a group of people they didn't know. Although they seemed to be insignificant, they were very important because they became the new inhabitants of the city.

Nehemiah 11:10–12 mentions a second group:

From the priests: Jedaiah the son of Joiarib, Jachin, Seraiah the son of Hilkiah, the son of Meshullam, the son of Zadok, the son of Meraioth, the son of Ahitub, the leader of the house of God, and their kinsmen who performed the work of the temple, 822.

Eight hundred and twenty-two people *willingly worked within the temple.* That's quite a staff! These people faithfully supported the work of the temple with their skills and gifts. The temple didn't have audio engineers, television technicians, lighting technicians, or structural engineers, as we have in some of our larger churches today; but you can be certain everyone in that group of eight hundred twenty-two had a very important job.

Nehemiah 11:15–16 tells us that the Levites and the "leaders of Levites" were *in charge of the outside work of the house of God.* In those days, "outside work" didn't just mean those who landscaped the temple grounds. Verse 16 refers to the leaders who worked outside the house of God, those who judged, handled civil affairs, and counseled and ministered to the public outside the place of worship. You probably can't remember one of their names! It's almost as if God has said, "I don't want you to remember those names." They are like those small white crosses in the cemetery. We remember them, not as individuals, but as a mass of willing workers who made it possible for important things to continue without a hitch.

Not a business today could exist for long without those extra-effort "nobodies" who diligently labor away from the limelight. These include the executive assistant who handles endless details; the custodian who keeps the place clean and neat; the human resources manager who interviews new people, listens to complaints, and keeps peace within the ranks; and the technicians and inspectors who work in windowless rooms to make sure a product meets certain standards.

A fourth "willing unknown" is revealed in verse 17: "Mattaniah [his genealogy follows] . . . was the leader in beginning the thanksgiving at *prayer*" (italics added). You probably didn't know Mattaniah ever existed! But God says he was a leader in prayer, both publicly and privately. He was likely a major cause for the success of the temple. He probably couldn't preach, teach, or sing; but the man could pray! As always, the unsung hero of the church is the kneeling saint.

If you haven't interacted with a person whose chief ministry is prayer, you have missed out on a great joy. When I first seriously considered entering ministry full time, I met an unusual woman in Houston. She had committed lengthy passages of Scripture to memory and could quote entire chapters of Isaiah and other prophets. When she wasn't in the Book, she was on her knees praying for others. But few people in her church even knew she was around.

This incredible woman literally prayed me through seminary. Then she prayed for me during my first experience in the gospel ministry. She supported my wife and me through the births of our four children and through the peaks and valleys of our lives. I can recite some amazing stories of God's provision for us through the years that I believe were a direct result of this woman's behind-the-scenes ministry on our behalf. You know my name because it's on the front of this book, but most people know nothing of this "willing unknown"—the *Mattaniah* of my life—who poured out her soul before the Lord on my behalf.

Finally, Nehemiah 11:22 tells us about the fifth unknown: *the singers for the services of the house of God.* The Living Bible says that the sons of Asaph were the "clan" that became the temple singers. Their role was to learn and rehearse music for worship services in the temple. They loved God and wanted to contribute their talent.

Do you remember these unknowns: the people who willingly moved into the city; the people who worked in the temple; the people who worked outside in related areas; the people who willingly prayed; and the people who sang in the services for God? All of them willingly gave of themselves.

MY FAVORITE ANONYMOUS PEOPLE

Even as I write this, my mind is flooded with the faces of those who worked behind the scenes over the years so that I could remain focused on the task of leadership. My wife faithfully and consistently supported me, encouraged me, worked with our children, and even took on the huge responsibility of leading our radio ministry, *Insight for Living.* I think of staff members who stuck with it day in and day out; the board members and officers who filled strategic roles while holding down full-time employment; the people who played instruments and sang in choirs in multiple services Sunday after Sunday; the people who prayed, who helped in the nursery, who taught, who worked in our library, who gave, who counseled, who visited; and gifted technicians who handled the sound systems, the lighting, and the tape recordings of every message. There are others who helped with parking, maintenance, and a host of other tasks that offer no tangible reward. Without them, my life would have been reduced to an endless list of tedious details that would have become the enemy of my ministry. I give God praise for each one of them who have willingly stood beside me without the benefit of public applause. With profound gratitude, I gladly declare their significance.

I am occasionally asked, "Who is your favorite Bible character?" I suppose most people expect me to say David or Elijah or Paul or Moses. And I do admire all of these great leaders. But many are surprised to hear me name people like Jabez, Amos, Abigail, Mephibosheth, Deborah, Epaphroditus, Onesiphorus, and Habakkuk. My questioners stare at me as if I've spoken in a foreign language! These people all were great men and women, and significant contributors to the success of Israel. But they also were virtually unknown, anonymous individuals. Each one, however, was an influential leader.

TIMELESS TRUTHS

We've spent considerable time dealing with many "willing unknowns." Now, putting all of it together, allow me to share some timeless truths with you. The first one is this: *Your gifts make you valuable, although not necessarily famous.* If you are gifted in an area that will never reach the spotlight, rest in the knowledge that you are as valuable to God's family as Mattaniah or Uzzi. Your work may be done anonymously, but you are not anonymous to God. And that fact introduces a second truth: *The Lord remembers every labor done in love.* With Him, nothing is ever forgotten. Take note of Hebrews 6:10:

> For God is not unjust so as to forget your work and the love
> which you have shown toward His name, in having ministered
> and in still ministering to the saints. (Hebrews 6:10)

Tuck Hebrews 6:10 into the back pocket of your mind and every
time you begin to feel discouraged because you don't receive the
recognition and affirmation you deserve, remember that God never
overlooks a single deed.

The third truth that I find in Nehemiah 11: *Our rewards will be
based on our faithfulness—not public applause.* The public may never
know of your ministry, but that will have nothing to do with final
rewards. God never checks an applause meter to measure the merit
of our service or to determine our rewards.

The day our family drove by the military cemetery in California
had a lasting impact on me. When I closed my eyes late that evening,
I could still envision the rows of white crosses standing guard over
the remains of dead heroes. I thought, "The dead are not silent; they
still speak." They reminded me that day, many years ago, and occasionally prompt me today to honor the large number of people who,
though unknown, still minister that a few might lead.

John McCrae closed his immortal poem with the reminder:

> Take up our quarrel with the foe:
> To you from failing hands we throw
> The torch; be yours to hold it high.
> If ye break faith with us who die
> We shall not sleep, though poppies grow
> In Flanders fields.[2]

May God genuinely encourage and stimulate every "willing unknown" who reads these words. And by the way, the poet knew what he was writing about. Lt. Col. John McCrae's body lies in a cemetery not far from Flanders fields, himself a quiet and virtually unknown hero of World War I.

Unknown, but not forgotten.

FIFTEEN

Happiness Is on the Wall

If happiness were a disease, none other would be more contagious. If you laugh often, if you're making life fun, if you're never very far from a smile, you'll have no trouble encouraging people and making friends. People who really enjoy life are always, *always* in demand.

Teachers who are happy and carry out their teaching in a winsome way have no trouble getting students to line up for their courses. A genuinely happy salesperson usually wins the incentive awards. When a college president is happy, the public relations department has a much easier job. When the owner and waitstaff of a restaurant are friendly and happy, the word spreads. Why? Because happiness is a rare commodity. In fact, it's almost extinct. If you question that, check out the drivers next time you're on the freeway. Most of them look like they could eat corn out of a Coke bottle.

I suppose it's understandable. The news channels are never short on bad news. National debt, terrorism, global warming, energy costs . . . and that's on the international and national level. That doesn't even include *local* bad news. Robbery, rape, pornography, traffic deaths, political scandals, kidnappings, rising taxes . . . And then there's personal bad news: so many families are crippled by marital infidelity, disease, spousal abuse, child abuse, substance abuse . . . lots of reasons to lose hope and adopt a pessimistic, cynical attitude in life.

People in health care professions are also extremely alarmed over the growing rate of suicide. It is now one of the major causes of death, especially among the young who cannot cope. One report claims: "Suicide is the third leading cause of death among young people ages 15 to 24."[1] Yet in spite of our current situation, God wants to set our hearts right concerning our day and age. I'm convinced He still finds delight when His people are joyful.

In the days of Nehemiah the people faced many depressing circumstances. They were, in fact, plagued with the most difficult times imaginable. Their situation did not inspire rejoicing. Nevertheless, many of them were filled with joy and laughter.

I'm not suggesting we become blissfully unaware of the problems that surround us as we glibly grin our way through hard times. However, I do think that Nehemiah 12 will help us discover how to lighten our load as we see things from God's perspective. I believe that we are marching toward the culmination of His divine plan—regardless of the suffering humanity must endure in the meantime. If we can think as God thinks and train ourselves to see life as He sees it, then we, as a community, can put the pain of life into perspective and learn to choose joy. I am convinced that this choice begins with a joyful leader.

Leaders need to be happy people! Those who look to a leader for encouragement and hope don't want the specter of the grim reaper sitting at the boss's desk. Many followers crawl to work every morning worn down by domestic conflicts and financial worries. They face a day of endless demands and thankless tasks, only later to return home to bickering, discontented mates and fussing children. Away from the job they have little more to look forward to than the glare of a television set. Somehow, if you are in a position to influence them, God can use you to introduce the one ingredient—real and lasting joy—that will lighten their load.

GATHERING THE RIGHT LEADERS

In Nehemiah 12:27, the people have gathered to dedicate the recently completed wall. The city was slowly beginning to show signs of progress—new homes, new businesses, the whole gamut of urban renewal. Although times were still hard, a new spark of enthusiasm and a renewed vision gave the people hope to continue what they had been doing—even though they had a long way to go. A monumental feat had been accomplished. The wall was finished: broad, stable, strong, carefully constructed and engineered. Having moved into the city and having begun to build their own homes, the citizens decided to dedicate the finished project to the Lord.

The dedication of the wall is the obvious subject of Nehemiah 12:27–47. But I want to highlight something just as important. Even though the people of Jerusalem had left their suburban comfort for the challenges of urban renewal, they carried with them a positive attitude, an infectious joy. Despite having to scrounge for building materials and basic resources, they considered the adventure a privilege. Why? How? Because they fixed their eyes on the Lord:

Now at the dedication of the wall of Jerusalem they sought out the Levites from all their places, to bring them to Jerusalem so that they might celebrate the dedication with gladness, with hymns of thanksgiving and with songs to the accompaniment of cymbals, harps and lyres. So the sons of the singers were assembled from the district around Jerusalem . . . (Nehemiah 12:27–28)

The Hebrew word for *gladness* means "gaiety, mirth, pleasure, delight." The people brought in this group of specialists and said, "Lead us in a joyful celebration! Let's have fun!" Then they added to the celebration by singing psalms and songs accompanied by cymbals, harps, and lyres. People from all around were selected to lead in the celebration of joy. It was designed to be an unforgettable, enjoyable day.

Clean Up Your Act!

The dedication consisted of more than fun and games, however. Notice something very important in verse 30: "The priests and the Levites purified themselves; they also purified the people, the gates and the wall." We must not overlook the fact that purification came before celebration. One commentator paints a vivid picture of what the ceremony might have looked like:

This ceremony of consecrating the wall and gates of the city was an act of piety on the part of Nehemiah, not merely to thank God in a general way for having been enabled to bring the building to a happy completion, but on the special ground of that city being the place which He had chosen, and its containing the temple which was hallowed by the manifestation of His presence, and anew set apart to His service. It was on these accounts that Jerusalem was called "the holy city," and by this public and solemn act of religious observance, after a long period of neglect and desecration, it was, as it were, restored to its rightful proprietor. The dedication consisted in a solemn ceremonial, in which the leading authorities, accompanied by the Levitical singers, summoned from all parts of the country, and by a vast concourse of people, marched in imposing procession round the city walls, and, pausing at intervals to engage in united praises, prayer, and sacrifices, supplicated the continued presence, favour, and blessing on "the holy city."[2]

In order to enjoy the city upon completion of the wall, their hearts had to be pure. By consecrating the wall, they consecrated themselves to the Lord. We, too, need to remember that to lead other people in a godly manner—whether in ministry, politics, the military, or business—our hearts must be clean before God. Holiness precedes happiness. Never forget that the first step to a happy countenance is a clean heart.

Not a single leader reading these words hasn't tried to fake a clean heart and failed. We know that moral carelessness and toying with sin give laughter a hollow ring. It's a deadly game. Mark it down. Any leader who expects his or her efforts to lift the spirits of others must start with a clean heart.

Everybody on the Wall!

Let's move ahead to the first procedure in the dedication ceremonies:

> Then I had the leaders of Judah come up on top of the wall, and
> I appointed two great choirs, the first proceeding to the right on
> top of the wall toward the Refuse Gate. (Nehemiah 12:31)

Picture that! Nehemiah ordered everyone on the wall and up they came by the dozens. The first great choir proceeded to Nehemiah's right, on top of the wall, toward the gate down at the bottom of the city, the Refuse Gate. Nehemiah tells us in Verse 38: "The second choir proceeded to the left, while I followed them with half of the people on the wall." Ezra led the first choir, while Nehemiah directed the second choir; so we have Ezra on one side of the city's wall and Nehemiah on the other side. I've often tried to imagine what that must have looked like from outside the wall. Hundreds of singers, all varieties of instruments, joyous dancing, and an elation that certainly wouldn't resemble today's average church service! That's what I get when I picture verse 43 in my mind: "On that day they offered great sacrifices and rejoiced because God had given them great joy, even the women and children rejoiced."

And they were loud! Verse 43 concludes, "the joy of Jerusalem was heard from afar." This reminds me of what it's like to arrive late to a football game as the roar of thousands and the band music build to a crescendo as you enter the stadium. The sheer energy and enthusiasm of that environment causes your heart to pound! The celebration in Jerusalem was like that. And leading the celebration were Nehemiah, Ezra, and the other leaders, all of them having a wonderful time.

Needed: Smiling, Singing Saints

The Bible says, "A joyful heart is good medicine" (Proverbs 17:22) and "A joyful heart makes a cheerful face, but when the heart is sad, the spirit is broken" (Proverbs 15:13). Isn't that the truth! People want to be near the individual who smiles and sings his or her way through life. I repeat: A joyful heart is contagious. And it fits any situation, no matter how bad the circumstances.

When I was in seminary, Cynthia and I lived in one of the campus apartments. Talk about a humble abode! (I'm happy to say those apartments have been torn down and replaced by a magnificent new library.) My study was so small that I had to step outside to turn a page. We had rats and the walls were so thin I used to harmonize with my neighbor as I showered. But we were determined we would cultivate our sense of humor instead of letting that tiny place paralyze us. Looking back, some of the most pleasant memories in our marriage occurred there. We entertained faculty members, fixed exotic meals (amazing what you can do with hamburger!), invited numerous couples and single students over, and even sang duets with the couple next door. We enjoyed it all four years!

How about you? Have you stopped singing? Have you stopped smiling and laughing at life? Why?

When you sing, your kids will sing too. And they won't care where they are! Years ago, I took our youngest son, Chuck, to a grocery store with me. We came up to the checkout stand to purchase a few items. For some reason, the store was abnormally quiet. Chuck, who was sitting in the cart, reached over and grabbed a handful of mints. While he was trying to unwrap one of them he began to sing in a loud voice, "Jesus loves me, this I know . . ." Everyone turned to stare at him. "For the Bible tells me so. Little ones . . ." His voice trailed off as he noticed a dozen eyes on him.

"Go ahead—'to Him belong,'" a young woman said to Chuck. Then she turned to me. "Do you know Christ as your Savior?"

"Why, yes, I do," I answered.

"I've been a Christian about a year and a half," she said.

A delightful conversation followed. My son's joy gave us an opportunity to encourage each other. I also discovered that the checkout clerk, who had stopped to listen, was discouraged over a broken marriage. Chuck's spontaneous outburst of melodic pleasure came at precisely the right moment. His happy little heart soothed the hurt of an otherwise sad adult.

Don't stop singing! Sing this afternoon. Sing on your way home from work. One of the most exuberant expressions of a happy heart is singing. (Glance at Ephesians 5:18–19.) I'm impressed with the fact that Nehemiah 12:43 does not say the song was heard from afar. It says, "the *joy* was heard from afar" (italics added). That encourages me! People don't pay much attention to voices and words, but they cannot ignore genuine, heartfelt joy.

The Secret: The Right Focus

One great application pours out of these verses: *Happiness is not dependent on outward circumstances but upon inward choice.* When you have chosen to focus on what's important in any situation, you can smile and sing through an experience and come out rejoicing. It all depends upon what you choose to make your focus.

My closing comments in this chapter go back to those of you who are now in leadership positions or plan to be in the future:

- Do you bring joy to those you lead?

- Is your leadership marked by a good sense of humor?

I know of few things more magnetic than a smile or a cheerful disposition, especially among those in God's work. How easy it is to become intense, severe, grim, and even oppressive! The people under Nehemiah's leadership felt free to rejoice and laugh. Do the people who are under your leadership feel that freedom? How about your children?

The Jews laughed on the wall as they rejoiced over God's provision. They sang together, and their joy flooded the hillside so all could hear and be glad. Had their circumstances changed? No, *they* had changed.

Have you?

Sixteen

Taking Problems by the Throat

The life of Ludwig van Beethoven, although one of great accomplishments, was checkered with sporadic agony. By the age of five, Beethoven played the violin under the tutelage of his father—also an accomplished musician. By thirteen, Beethoven had become an accomplished concert organist. By the age of twenty, he had studied under the very capable hands of Joseph Haydn and the gifted mentor, W. A. Mozart. In fact, Mozart spoke prophetic words when he declared that Beethoven would give the world something worth listening to by the time his life ended.

As Beethoven began to develop his skills, he became a prolific composer. During his lifetime, he wrote nine majestic symphonies and five concertos for piano, not to mention numerous pieces of chamber music. Ludwig van Beethoven also wrote numerous sonatas and pieces for violin and piano. He has thrilled us with the masterful works of unique harmony that broke with the traditions of his times. The man was a genius.

Beethoven was not, however, a stranger to difficulties. During his twenties, he began to lose his hearing. His fingers "became thick," he said on one occasion. He couldn't feel the music as he once had been able to do. His hearing problem haunted him in the middle years of his life, but he kept it a well-guarded secret. By his fifties, Beethoven was stone deaf, nevertheless he continued to compose. He conducted the premiere of his great Ninth Symphony to thunderous applause, of which he was completely unaware until someone made him turn around. Four years later, he contracted pneumonia and never completely recovered. He remained bedridden for several months before dying from cirrhosis of the liver.

He was deaf, and yet a magnificent musician. In a letter to a friend, Beethoven wrote, "I will seize Fate by the throat; it will certainly not bend and crush me completely—Oh, it would be so lovely to live a thousand lives."[1] He had determined not to give in. Many of his biographers feel that because of his great determination, Beethoven remained far more productive than he otherwise would have been. Indeed, he took life by the throat.

I would like to borrow that phrase and apply it to leadership. I won't dwell on such things as physical infirmity, though some today may wrestle with similar maladies—perhaps secrets known only by you and God. I will apply Beethoven's phrase to the areas of wrong that we must face and "take by the throat." Our main character will not be Beethoven, but Nehemiah in the final chapter of his book.

Nehemiah faced four great problems that he "took by the throat." He was determined not to let them conquer him or the people he served.

UNDERSTANDING THE BACKGROUND

For a period of time following the dedication of the wall, Nehemiah continued to establish a righteous government in Jerusalem. Eventually, we learn in verse 6, he left the city and went back to his first assignment as a cupbearer to the king. We also become aware that certain things took place while he was gone:

> But during all this time [the time described in verses 1–5] I was not in Jerusalem, for in the thirty-second year of Artaxerxes king of Babylon I had gone to the king. After some time, however, I asked leave from the king. (Nehemiah 13:6)

We don't know how long Nehemiah was absent from Jerusalem. But while the cat was away, the rats were busy making havoc in the city! When he returned, Nehemiah discovered four significant problems that demanded correction. And his approach was nothing less than direct as he took each one by the throat.

Compromising Companionship

Nehemiah 13:4–9 describes the first problem, which I'll label *the problem of a compromising companionship*. To appreciate it, you have to understand the main characters involved.

Prior to Nehemiah's return, Eliashib (the priest who was appointed over the chambers of the house of God and who was a relative of Tobiah) had prepared a large room for Tobiah. We do not know much about these two men. Later on, Eliashib is called "the high priest." He was responsible for the vessels and the rooms, and the worship in the house of God. Eliashib had planned to set aside part of a chamber in the house of God to be a residence for Tobiah.

Tobiah, as recorded in the book, had remained an enemy of God and a frequent thorn in Nehemiah's side. Nehemiah had faced him repeatedly as Tobiah had tried to stop construction of the wall and had personally criticized, attacked, and assaulted Nehemiah. But all the way through his Jerusalem project, Nehemiah made sure that Tobiah never got inside the walls. Tobiah is the classic example of the darkened unbeliever or the rebellious, carnal Christian who tries every possible way to undermine the work of God. His resistance was relentless.

However, while Nehemiah was away Eliashib had said, "Let's prepare a room for Tobiah" (Nehemiah 13:5). You see, in those days, the house of God was different than the church of today. It was joined by chambers—large rooms that often held grain or utensils or vessels for worship. So Eliashib had said, "Let's clear out the area normally given to this storage and provide a nice room for Tobiah. Let's bring him in. He has been rejected long enough. Let's allow him to stay in the courts, to live in one of the chambers." Verse 9 even suggests that he had a suite of rooms: "I gave an order and they cleansed the rooms." (Notice the plural.)

Now prior to this, Eliashib the priest, who was appointed over the chambers of the house of our God, being related to Tobiah, had prepared a large room for him, where formerly they put the grain offerings, the frankincense, the utensils and the tithes of grain, wine and oil prescribed for the Levites, the singers and the gatekeepers, and the contributions for the priests. (Nehemiah 13:4–5)

Verse 6 explains that Nehemiah had been away. Then, in verse 7, he writes, "I came to Jerusalem and learned about the evil that Eliashib had done for Tobiah, by preparing a room for him in the courts of the house of God." In short, Nehemiah came back to Jerusalem and found that the house of God had been infiltrated by Tobiah and his evil plans. So, Nehemiah did what any good leader would do; he took the problem by the throat!

Verse 8 says: "It was very displeasing to me . . ." Nehemiah is careful to give us, first of all, his attitude toward evil before he tells us the action he took against it. "I threw all of Tobiah's household goods out of the room."

It's remarkable how practical—even earthy—God's Word can be! People who envision these saints of the Old Testament with halos and flowing robes have missed the whole point of the narrative. Nehemiah went into the rooms and threw all of Tobiah's gear out into the streets. Having Tobiah in the house of God was a violation of the worst kind. His questionable heritage cast doubt on his being a Jew, to say nothing of being a Levite. He was an Ammonite who married into the community and had numerous political connections, including the royal house in Babylon.

I love verse 9 because it's so vivid. "Then I gave an order and they cleansed the rooms." He makes it sound as though they fumigated the place. Nehemiah didn't want even the smell of Tobiah hanging in the air of God's house.

Isn't it interesting that we really don't know how to get mad about the right things? Too often we jump and scream about the wrong things. Now, you'll never convince me in a thousand years that Nehemiah folded his hands and said, "Tsk, tsk, now that is a shame.

My, oh my . . . we must pray about what we should do with Tobiah's nice belongings." No! He opened that door and said, "Haul that stuff out!" They got rid of Tobiah's belongings, and when the room was stripped clean, swept out, and ready, they brought in the grain (see Nehemiah 13:9). Can you imagine Tobiah coming home that night to a room full of grain?

Nehemiah did that because he was determined he would not live with *wrong* (Tobiah's evil) in a place that was built for *right*. Some people still have not become convinced of that. God's leaders must constantly guard against compromise. In so many words, Nehemiah said, "Leadership is not a popularity contest. I won't pander to political pressure from the nobles, and I'm not afraid to face Artaxerxes. My priority is cleansing God's house of evil's contamination."

FINANCIAL FIASCO

The next problem Nehemiah faced (revealed in Nehemiah 13:10–14) I'll call *the problem of a financial fiasco*. I like the way verse 10 begins: "I also discovered." That tells me that he was looking. A leader keeps his eyes open! Nehemiah discovered something else that was wrong.

> The portions of the Levites had not been given them, so that the Levites and the singers who performed the service had gone away, each to his own field. (Nehemiah 13:10)

In those days the people who served in the temple were called Levites and drew their living from the temple. People who sang there were supported by the people who attended. Worshipers brought offerings of meat and produce from their farms, part of which was given to sustain the temple workers. But Nehemiah returned to Jerusalem and found that the singers and the Levites had to return to their farming in order to eat.

Take note of Nehemiah's response:

> I reprimanded the officials and said, "Why is the house of God forsaken?" Then I gathered them together and restored them to their posts. (Nehemiah 13:11)

His ejection of Tobiah had already ruffled a few political feathers; this would only agitate his enemies further. Nevertheless, he continued to say, "This is wrong. God requires in the law a paying of the tithe, and you're not doing it." And I strongly suspect that Nehemiah raised his voice in this verbal rebuke to the officials. Then he devised a plan for change and immediately put it into operation.

Finally, he prayed:

> Remember me for this, O my God, and do not blot out my loyal deeds which I have performed for the house of my God and its services. (Nehemiah 13:14)

I firmly believe in the importance of prayer. Sometimes prayer is the only appropriate response to certain problems. And then there are situations in which prayer can become a cop-out. When direct disobedience has caused problems, a prayer of repentance is a fine beginning, but only a beginning. *Obedience is needed.* And that calls for action!

There are times when we traffic in the realm of wrong. When this occurs, God does not expect His child merely to fall to his knees and offer long confessions or petitions. He says in effect, "Get off your knees and go about the business of correcting the wrong." This is what I find in the story of Nehemiah. And it is applicable for today. It's all part of taking problems by the throat.

Some of you may need to take a long look at what God's Word teaches about giving. You may need to carefully evaluate just what part God is playing in your giving plans. If you were to compile a list of things that make up your expenditures, where would the Lord's part be? Would it be toward the bottom or toward the top? Shouldn't His part be first? All that we are and all that we have and hope to be comes down from His gracious hands. A grateful Christian is a generous Christian.

SECULARIZED SABBATH

Nehemiah 13:15–22 reports a third problem that Nehemiah grabbed by the throat. I will call it *the problem of the secularized Sabbath.*

> In those days I saw in Judah some who were treading wine presses on the sabbath, and bringing in sacks of grain and loading them on donkeys, as well as wine, grapes, figs and all kinds of loads, and they brought them into Jerusalem on the sabbath day . . . (Nehemiah 13:15)

In the Jewish system the Sabbath, Saturday, was (and still is) a day of rest and reflection. It was a day set aside by the Lord for His people, the Jews, to focus their attention on their Creator.

The people made a covenantal promise to God in Nehemiah 10:31. They recorded their promise and they sealed it with their signatures. They said,

> As for the peoples of the land who bring wares or any grain on the sabbath day to sell, we will not buy from them on the sabbath or a holy day; and we will forego the crops the seventh year and the exaction of every debt. (Nehemiah 10:31)

In other words, the people said they would observe—to the letter—a literal day of rest.

As Nehemiah was walking through the city, he saw that the merchants were back to their old tricks. Grain was still being sold on the Sabbath. Loads were being brought in through the gates and taken back out. Profit making, expenditures of monies, and the receiving of goods—all were taking place on the Sabbath. Nehemiah must have shaken his head in disappointment. The people's covenantal promise was still fresh in his memory.

> So I admonished them on the day they sold food. Also men of Tyre were living there who imported fish and all kinds of merchandise, and sold them to the sons of Judah on the sabbath, even in Jerusalem. (Nehemiah 13:15–16)

The Lord didn't forbid His people to make a profit and saw nothing wrong with their having a good business. However, if you were a Jew, *none of that was appropriate on the Sabbath.*

As he did before, Nehemiah took the problem by the throat.

Then I reprimanded the nobles of Judah and said to them, "What is this evil thing you are doing, by profaning the sabbath day? . . . It came about that just as it grew dark at the gates of Jerusalem before the sabbath, I commanded that the doors should be shut and that they should not open them until after the sabbath. Then I stationed some of my servants at the gates so that no load would enter on the sabbath day. (Nehemiah 13:17, 19)

The Jews then, as now, considered sundown the beginning of the next day. So at roughly six o'clock on Friday evening, the Sabbath began. They were to take a full day's break from commerce and the routine of workaday life to enjoy their relationship with God. Nehemiah observed the sun beginning to set and said, "Shut the gates. The sabbath is here." And to prevent cheating, he posted guards.

I love the next two verses.

Once or twice the traders and merchants of every kind of merchandise spent the night outside Jerusalem. (Nehemiah 13:20)

Nehemiah didn't win many friends among the fellows who had fish to trade. But that didn't bother him.

Then I warned them and said to them, "Why do you spend the night in front of the wall? If you do so again, I will use force against you." From that time on they did not come on the sabbath. (Nehemiah 13:21)

His aggressive plan worked! Nehemiah knew what issues

deserved righteous anger and when to exercise restraint. He knew where he stood on the issue of a *secularized Sabbath* and he held his ground. Nehemiah said, "Don't come back on the Sabbath. Saturday is the day we honor our God."

You may have a conviction God has given you. If this is the case, you had better carry it out. You'd better have the grit to say, "No, I will not" or, "Yes, I will continue" because there will always be individuals who will try to change your standards to fit theirs. You'll need to take that problem by the throat. Don't mess around . . . talk straight . . . do what's right.

For example, I know of an outstanding Christian educator who had just taken over the presidency of one of the most secularist colleges in the nation. On the day he interviewed for the position, he stated very clearly that should his responsibilities on the job interfere with his prior commitment to Christ and His kingdom, his loyalty to the latter would take precedence. He stated his case honestly . . . and he got the job. How we need more men and women of similar conviction!

By the way, let me pause a moment to add this thought: I have rarely known anyone who uprooted a deep-seated wrong without first becoming sufficiently angry. Spirit-filled anger can stir up motivation. We need to declare an all-out war against wrong in our personal lives. Anything less than that won't be effective.

DOMESTIC DISOBEDIENCE

The fourth and final problem Nehemiah confronted is perhaps the most difficult of all the problems he faced. Nehemiah, once again, declared war against *the problem of domestic disobedience.* Nehemiah

13:23 says; "In those days I also saw that the Jews had married women from Ashdod, Ammon and Moab."

The Jews were supposed to refrain from intermarriage with Gentiles in order to avoid polluting their homes with idolatry. The men had married women who worshiped false gods and their children were being taught nothing about God.

> As for their children, half spoke in the language of Ashdod, and none of them was able to speak the language of Judah, but the language of his own people. (Nehemiah 13:24)

Hebrew was the language of Scripture, so the children could glean nothing from the reading of God's Word. And this, again, brought Nehemiah's righteous anger to the boiling point.

> So I contended with them and cursed them and struck some of them and pulled out their hair, and made them swear by God, "You shall not give your daughters to their sons, nor take of their daughters for your sons or for yourselves." (Nehemiah 13:25)

Cursing in this context does not mean he used coarse profanity. Rather, it means "to be disrespectful, to dishonor." It's a severe term, implying "to treat with contempt, to revile." He also "struck some of them and pulled out their hair." The Hebrew word translated pulled out their hair means "to make bald, to make slick or polished." It usually referred to the beard, a plucking out of part of the beard.

We are so careful, so tactful, so diplomatic. Sometimes, too much so! We are afraid to confront. Our lives skate along, glazed with compromise and tolerance. Often at the heart of a compounded, complex matter, we're afraid to say honestly to someone, "You know something? You never did take care of that issue back there, did you?" Or, "You know what? Selfishness is at the heart of the problem you're wrestling with." Nehemiah was not afraid to pluck out beards for the sake of right. When you stop and think about it, he *literally* took that problem by the throat!

If you know about something in your domestic life that's in violation of what you know God has commanded, take that problem by the throat—*do* something about it. Your personal life is so important to God. He longs to direct your steps. If you are careless, all sorts of "Tobiahs," such as "financial selfishness" will cause you to stray from the path the Lord has planned for you. All those areas of rest God wants to give you, you will fill up with worry and you will secularize what the Lord has made sacred. By and by, these things will consume your entire life.

In the last verses of Nehemiah's "memoirs," he comes before God in prayer, saying, "Remember me, my God. I have only their good at heart."

Overcoming Passivity

While attending a conference decades ago, I was impressed with a statement made by Dr. Art Glasser: "Passivity is an enemy."

These words have rung in my ears for more than forty years. As I try to express Nehemiah's closing message to leaders, that statement seems to say it best. No leader dare play around with wrong. It must be taken by the throat. Passivity is, and remains, an enemy.

Look at how Nehemiah took passivity by the throat:

1. *Nehemiah faced the wrong head-on.* I've never known a wrong to be solved until it is admitted to be just that—a wrong. When Nehemiah learned of wrong, he faced the situation head-on. If you have a problem in your church, your business, your home—anywhere in your life—face it head-on. Don't skirt it. Sure, it will be painful, but deal with it. Start today.

2. *Nehemiah dealt with the wrong severely.* After seeing the wrong or the problem as it really was, he dealt with it severely. I'm sure some people said, "Man, Nehemiah, you're getting cranky. You used to relax a lot more than you do now." And I'm just as sure that Nehemiah must have thought, "I don't care. I answer to God!" Our lives must not be politically swayed by the applause or wishes of the public. That's really difficult because it's hard to stand against wrong and not appear to be a crotchety old crank. But Nehemiah stood firm. He didn't pick a fight; he just dealt with sin severely. Any leader who expects to be respected must do the same.

3. *Nehemiah worked toward a permanent correction.* It's not enough just to condemn the wrong. You must do something to correct it. I'm thrilled with the way God communicates this in the Bible. Whenever God says, "Don't do this," He backs it up with, "Do that instead." God always balances a negative with a positive. So it must be in our lives. When you take some wrong by the throat and plan to get rid of it, replace it with something better.

4. *Nehemiah always followed up the wrong with prayer.* When Nehemiah had done all that he could, he fell before God and said, "Oh, God, bless every one of these efforts. Give me direction and more wisdom and guidance. Remember me as I have done all I can to correct the wrong. Honor Yourself as I stand alone."

HONESTY ... CONVICTION ... DEVOTION

Three brief applications form Nehemiah's final counsel to leaders.

First, *taking any problem by the throat starts with an honest observation.* Detection precedes solution. You can never solve a problem you cannot define. You must define it; call it what it is. The problem may be a compromising alliance that you have begun—in your business, in your social life, perhaps in your dating life. Maybe you've begun to let go of the reins of responsibility. Whatever the wrong in your life may be, it's bound to take its toll on you.

Do you remember Samson? He walked so far away from God that when God's Spirit finally departed from him, Samson didn't even know it. The old King James Version says, "He wist not that the Lord was departed from him" (Judges 16:20). Erosion was at work. Samson had lived a lie so long and his leadership had become so dishonest that he failed to see the full impact of his compromising lifestyle.

Honest observation must come first.

Second, *the honest observation must be matched with courageous conviction.* Any leader who determines to live a godly life is going to have to brace himself with conviction. A godly walk requires a fearless determination and the taking of strong measures to stand firm.

In the spiritual realm we cannot tolerate everybody doing his own thing. If we do, our Christian conviction weakens. I'm not saying we should never bend. I'm not advocating blind intolerance. I am saying that it is the responsibility of leaders, who determine to be thoroughly Christian, to stand firm in spite of those who don't agree. You will never be popular if you do that, especially with those who don't like the way you're laying the bricks.

Joshua said, "Choose for yourselves today whom you will serve" (Joshua 24:15). Notice Joshua did not say, "Shall we discuss this idea? Would you like to talk it over?" He said, in effect, "That's it!" A leader must declare courageous convictions.

Third, *honest observation and courageous conviction must be tempered with deep devotion.* This is where many well-meaning Christians miss it. They become cynical savages: negative, angry, witch-hunting Christians who are always suspicious and frequently fighting. Their joy of the Lord is replaced with a long, deep frown. The leader must maintain a balance between standing for the truth and keeping his heart warm before the Lord.

I think it is significant that the final scene in Nehemiah's book portrays him on his knees asking God for grace. He had fought hard for the right, but he had kept his heart soft before the Lord. What a magnificent model of leadership! He was a man of honesty, conviction, and devotion.

Our world has lost its way. It is filled with a fearful and confused humanity. Shepherdless sheep by the millions long for a voice of assurance, a cause to believe in, an authentic model to follow. They seek for someone to calm their fears, to resolve their confusion, to channel their energies. They are calling for strong-minded, warm-hearted leaders.

Will you be one of them?

If so, you must take life by the throat.

NOTES

Chapter 1

1. John Bartlett, *Familiar Quotations* (Boston: Little, Brown and Company, 1951), 708.
2. Merrill F. Unger, *Unger's Bible Dictionary* (Chicago: Moody Press, 1959), 230.
3. Reprinted from *The Root of the Righteous* by A. W. Tozer, copyright 1986 by Zur Ltd. Used by permission of WingSpread Publishers, a division of Zur Ltd. 800-885-4571.

Chapter 2

1. Alan Redpath, *Victorious Christian Service* (Grand Rapids, MI: Fleming H. Revell, a division of Baker Book, 1994).
2. "Got Any Rivers" by Oscar Eliason. Copyright © 1945 Singspiration Music (ASCAP), (Administered by Brentwood-Benson Music Publishing, Inc .). All rights reserved. Used by permission.

Chapter 4

1. Winston Churchill, *Never Give In!: The Best of Winston Churchill's Speeches,* ed. Winston S. Churchill (New York: Hyperion, 2003), 206.
2. *Ibid.,* 218.
3. John Bartlett, *Familiar Quotations* (Boston: Little, Brown and Company, 1951), 851.

Chapter 5

1. J. Oswald Sanders, *Spiritual Leadership* (Chicago: Moody Press, 1967), 110.
2. J. B. Phillips, *Letters to Young Churches* (New York: Macmillan, 1955), 76.

3. Theodore Roosevelt, "The Man in the Arena (Citizenship in a Republic)," in *Theodore Roosevelt: Letters and Speeches,* ed. Louis Auchincloss (New York: Library of America, 2004), 781–782.
4. Theodore Roosevelt, "The Strenuous Life," in *Theodore Roosevelt: Letters and Speeches,* ed. Louis Auchincloss (New York: Library of America, 2004), 757.

Chapter 6
1. John Edmund Haggai, *How to Win Over Worry* (Grand Rapids: Harvest House, 2004).
2. Charles Edison, "The Electric Thomas Edison," in *Great Lives, Great Deeds* (New York: Reader's Digest Association, 1964), 203.
3. Charles Haddon Spurgeon quoted in Helmut Thielicke, *Encounter with Spurgeon,* trans. John W. Doberstein (Philadelphia: Fortress Press, 1963), 219.

Chapter 7
1. Clarence E. Macartney, *Preaching without Notes* (Nashville: Abingdon Press, 1946), 178.

Chapter 8
1. John Bartlett, *Familiar Quotations* (Boston: Little, Brown and Company, 1951), 381.
2. G. Frederick Owen, *Abraham to the Middle-East Crisis* (Grand Rapids: Eerdmans, 1957), 56–57.
3. J. Oswald Sanders, *Spiritual Leadership* (Chicago: Moody Press, 1967), 64.

Chapter 9
1. Gilbert K. Chesterton, *What's Wrong with the World* (New York: Dodd, Mead and Company, 1910), 48.
2. Gerrit Verkuyl, ed., *The Modern Language Bible, The New Berkley Version* (Grand Rapids: Zondervan, 1969), 208.

Chapter 10
1. Peter F. Drucker, *Management* (New York: Harper & Row, 1974), 301–302.
2. Ordway Tead, *The Art of Leadership* (New York: McGraw-Hill, 1935), 215.

Chapter 12
1. Søren Kierkegaard, *Purity of Heart*, rev. ed., trans. Douglas V. Steere (New York: Harper, 1948), 51.
2. A.W. Tozer, *The Knowledge of the Holy* (New York: Harper, 1978).
3. Richard Chenevix Trench quoted in *The Kneeling Christian* (Grand Rapids: Zondervan Publishing House, 1945), 52.

Chapter 13
1. Billy Graham, *World Aflame* (New York: Doubleday, 1965), 22–23.
2. Keith Miller, *The Taste of New Wine* (Orleans, MA: Paraclete, 1993).

Chapter 14
1. John McCrae, "In Flanders Fields" in *Modern British Poetry*, ed. Louis Untermeyer (New York: Harcourt, 1920), 101.
2. *Ibid.*

Chapter 15
1. Centers for Disease Control and Prevention, "Suicide: Fact Sheet," n.p. [cited 30 Aug. 2006]. Online: http://www.cdc.gov/ncipc/factsheets/suifacts.htm.
2. Robert Jamieson, A. R. Fausset, and David Brown, *A Commentary, Critical and Explanatory, on the Old and New Testaments* (New York: Richard R. Smith, Inc., 1930), Neh. 12:27.

Chapter 16
1. Lewis Lockwood, *Beethoven: The Music and the Life* (New York: W.W. Norton & Company, Inc., 2005), 115.